Editor-in-Chief and Founder:
   Lyndon H. LaRouche, Jr.
Editorial Board: *Lyndon H. LaRouche, Jr. , Helga Zepp-LaRouche, Robert Ingraham, Tony Papert, Gerald Rose, Dennis Small, Jeffrey Steinberg, William Wertz*
Co-Editors: *Robert Ingraham, Tony Papert*
Managing Editor: *Nancy Spannaus*
Technology: *Marsha Freeman*
Books: *Katherine Notley*
Ebooks: *Richard Burden*
Graphics: *Alan Yue*
Photos: *Stuart Lewis*
Circulation Manager: *Stanley Ezrol*

INTELLIGENCE DIRECTORS
Counterintelligence: *Jeffrey Steinberg, Michele Steinberg*
Economics: *John Hoefle, Marcia Merry Baker, Paul Gallagher*
History: *Anton Chaitkin*
Ibero-America: *Dennis Small*
Russia and Eastern Europe: *Rachel Douglas*
United States: *Debra Freeman*

INTERNATIONAL BUREAUS
Bogotá: *Miriam Redondo*
Berlin: *Rainer Apel*
Copenhagen: *Tom Gillesberg*
Houston: *Harley Schlanger*
Lima: *Sara Madueño*
Melbourne: *Robert Barwick*
Mexico City: *Gerardo Castilleja Chávez*
New Delhi: *Ramtanu Maitra*
Paris: *Christine Bierre*
Stockholm: *Ulf Sandmark*
United Nations, N.Y.C.: *Leni Rubinstein*
Washington, D.C.: *William Jones*
Wiesbaden: *Göran Haglund*

ON THE WEB
e-mail: eirns@larouchepub.com
www.larouchepub.com
www.executiveintelligencereview.com
www.larouchepub.com/eiw
Webmaster: *John Sigerson*
Assistant Webmaster: *George Hollis*
Editor, Arabic-language edition: *Hussein Askary*

EIR (ISSN 0273-6314) *is published weekly (50 issues), by EIR News Service, Inc., P.O. Box 17390, Washington, D.C. 20041-0390. (703) 777-9451*

European Headquarters: E.I.R. GmbH, Postfach Bahnstrasse 9a, D-65205, Wiesbaden, Germany Tel: 49-611-73650
Homepage: http://www.eirna.com
e-mail: eirna@eirna.com
Director: Georg Neudecker

Montreal, Canada: 514-461-1557

Denmark: EIR - Danmark, Sankt Knuds Vej 11, basement left, DK-1903 Frederiksberg, Denmark. Tel.: +45 35 43 60 40, Fax: +45 35 43 87 57. e-mail: eirdk@hotmail.com.

Mexico City: EIR, Sor Juana Inés de la Cruz 242-2 Col. Agricultura C.P. 11360 Delegación M. Hidalgo, México D.F. Tel. (5525) 5318-2301 eirmexico@gmail.com

Postmaster: Send all address changes to *EIR*, P.O. Box 17390, Washington, D.C. 20041-0390.

Signed articles in *EIR* represent the views of the authors, and not necessarily those of the Editorial Board.

The Only Way Out

No Solution But To Shut Down Wall Street Now

Jan. 11—Mass deaths and economic devastation are now on the immediate agenda for the population of the United States, as well as Europe, as the effect of Wall Street's policy as implemented under the Obama Presidency. "There is no possibility of keeping people alive, under the present trends of conditions," Lyndon La-Rouche warned in a discussion with the LPAC Policy Committee today, emphasizing that the collapse of the international financial system of which he had warned in mid-December, is fully underway.

"Your economic policy of the United States, and of the British Empire in general, demands the immediate mass genocide of the people of the trans-Atlantic community," LaRouche stated. "That's a fact! If we expose that now, we still have a last moment of chance to reverse that effect by shutting down Wall Street and removing Obama from office."

The fact is, that every single dollar of Wall Street's $2 quadrillion speculative bubble is totally worthless, and must be wiped off the books without recompense. Otherwise, under the "bail-in" policy now being implemented, everything you and your family may have—savings, pensions, food, health care, jobs, homes, everything—will be seized in the name of protecting the criminal British Empire system which created that speculative bubble.

Therefore, Wall Street has to be shut down *now*, LaRouche insists, and Franklin Roosevelt's Glass-Steagall law reinstated. That then has to be followed up with a supporting action, a Franklin Roosevelt solution, "to organize mass funding for people who have lost their sources of income; for people who have been tortured to death" by lack of food and the conditions under which they live and work.

"The people must also know that there's a hope of reversing the kind of treatment of their employment—or non-employment—which is hitting the people today, as in the early 1930s, when Franklin Roosevelt moved in, to give the people a hope of existence."

LaRouche pointed to the actual root of the problem: that people fell for the lie that money is actual wealth, and an entire financial system has been built on that lie. But, "money is not something which has a self-evident value. Value depends upon the creative powers of mankind, to make better the conditions of life of mankind."

Death Spiral

LaRouche issued this clarion call to arms on Jan. 11, even as the trans-Atlantic financial system was sinking into a death spiral. In the first week of 2016, global markets crashed by 6.5%, wiping out $4 trillion in worthless paper; the price of oil plunged by 10%, and is now headed to under $30 per barrel; Puerto Rico defaulted

LaRouche PAC
Lyndon LaRouche, addressing the Manhattan Project on September 26, 2015.

on a chunk of its $72 billion debt, which could create a crisis that could quickly spread throughout the entire municipal bond market; and the Jan. 1 activation of the British Empire's bail-in policy across Europe is leading to a freezing-up of the bond market, with early indications that even inter-bank lending is seizing up.

Lyndon LaRouche, the world's leading economic forecaster, had warned in mid-December that precisely this would occur. In a statement that was widely circulated internationally, LaRouche on Dec. 17 warned that the planet stood at the edge of the abyss of a general collapse of the trans-Atlantic system, and that this would strike "shortly after the first of this next year." He stated that the British Empire's policies under these conditions, especially its bail-in thievery of trillions of dollars of citizens' assets, scheduled to go into high gear in Europe on Jan. 1, would unleash genocide on a level not seen since the Fourteenth Century New Dark Age, which wiped out nearly half of the European population. And he warned that this general collapse would happen suddenly, as it now is.

Do not look for the cause of the crisis in proximate *effects*, such as Puerto Rico's default, the blow-out of the shale-oil and related bubbles, or in the Federal Reserve's incompetent decision to raise interest rates by 0.25% in December. And for sure don't be so imbecilic as to blame China for the meltdown of the trans-Atlantic financial system, supposedly because its GDP growth rate for 2015 came in at "only" 6.9%, as compared to an expected 7%. Asia, led by China, is the only sector of the world economy which is doing relatively well in physical economic terms today, and will be partially—but only partially—shielded from the trans-Atlantic meltdown.

The cause of the financial events now unfolding is to be found in the gargantuan, completely unpayable $2 quadrillion speculative bubble that has built up across all markets since the demise of the Glass-Steagall Law in 1999, and in the underlying belief that *money*, and *money alone*, constitutes real wealth. To that, add the concomitant policy of *negative economic growth* and drastic population reduction, which is the stated policy of the British Empire and of its stooge Obama.

Quantitative Stealing

Take the case of the so-called bail-in policy which went into effect across the European Union on Jan. 1, 2016, and is also fully authorized in the United States under Title II of the criminal Dodd-Frank bill passed by Congress in 2010—under excruciating pressure and

blackmail from Barack Obama, and in opposition to the Glass-Steagall policy that the concerted campaign of the LaRouche Movement had succeeded in getting placed on Congress's agenda at that time.

Bail-in has been sold to the public as the way to make sure that another Lehman-style 2008 financial crisis never occurs. Instead of using government funds to *bail out* failing banks through Quantitative Easing and similar hyperinflationary measures, the bankrupt banks purportedly will instead be kept afloat by a *bail-in* of certain categories of deposits in the banks, and certain categories of bonds of the banks. In other words, depositors and *some* investors will be *expropriated*, in order to salvage the cancerous financial bubble. This is what was done in Cyprus when its banks went belly-up in 2013, and it was then promoted as the "Cyprus template" for all of Europe by Eurogroup President Jeroen Dijsselbloem.

At the time, *EIR* dubbed the bail-in hoax nothing more than "Quantitative Stealing." We also noted that one man's *bail-in* is another man's *bail-out*. The crucial question is, what financial instruments are meant to be bailed out, or kept afloat, by the Quantitative Stealing of others? The answer is explicit, in both the EU's guidelines for so-called "bank resolution" and in Obama's Dodd-Frank law: Derivatives held by the world's megabanks are not to be touched, if doing so would create "systemic" problems for the international financial system—which, of course, would be the case in all instances. The plan, in other words, is to rob Peter (you and your family) to pay Paul (Wall Street and the City of London).

But the scheme is absurd even on its own terms. There are about $1.5 quadrillion in financial derivatives in existence, out of a total $2 quadrillion financial bubble. How much loot is available to be bailed in to salvage the derivatives? A "mere" $16 trillion,[1] scarcely

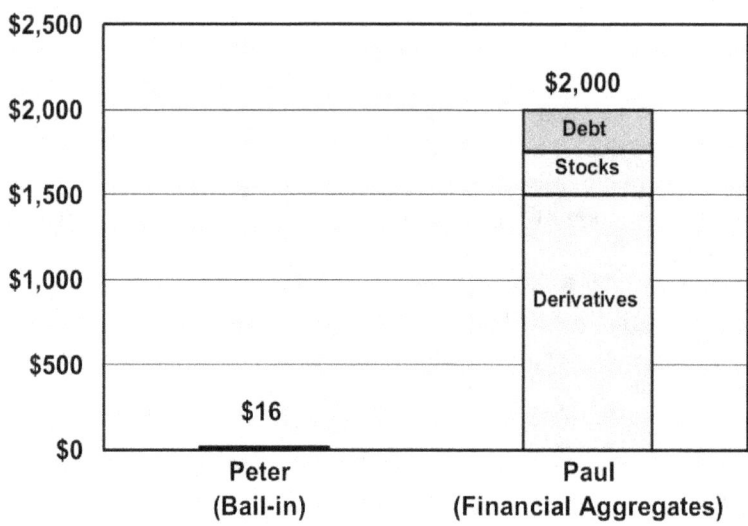

FIGURE 1

The Fraud of Bail-In: Robbing Peter To Pay Paul

(trillions $)

1% the size of the derivatives bubble that Wall Street intends to rescue! (see **Figure 1**)

By no stretch of the imagination can this cockamamie scheme work for its stated purpose of salvaging the financial bubble. The only result of Wall Street's bail-in policy in the real world will be to accelerate the onrushing financial meltdown and totally destroy the physical economy and the population's living standard, leading to rapidly accelerating death rates across the planet—which is precisely the stated intent of the British Empire.

Jail, not Bail

What is now referred to as "bail-in" used to be called by its proper name: *fraud*. Back in the 1920s and 1930s, JP Morgan and other banks knowingly defrauded their clients by pushing them to buy shares in their banks, which shortly went belly-up. Some bankers went to jail for the crime back then—courtesy of FDR. A few years ago, Spain's major banks, including Banco Santander, pulled the same stunt by selling their own clients so-called "preferentes" (preferred) shares in the failing

---

1. In the case of the EU, the guidelines that went into effect on Jan. 1 require banks to issue so-called "bail-in bonds" equal to 8% of their total assets. Bail-in bonds are self-defined as bonds that would be instantly expropriated when a bank becomes insolvent—in other words, they are rat poison. Leaving aside for a moment who in the world would ever buy such a guaranteed-to-fail financial instrument, the total amount to be issued in the EU is about $2.8 trillion (8% of the $34.5 trillion in bank assets). If a similar approach is taken in Japan and the U.S. (where it is also mandated, under Dodd-Frank), another $1.9 trillion in such bonds would be issued, for a total of $4.7 trillion globally.

If you add to that bail-in amount, the outright seizure and expropriation of bank deposits as was done in Cyprus (about one-third of the total, despite pious promises from EU authorities that deposits of under 100,000 euros would not be touched, promises which were promptly violated), that theoretically would add another $11.8 trillion to the pot of assets to be stolen. So the nominal total bail-in would be slightly over $16 trillion—nowhere near enough to salvage the derivatives bubble, but plenty big enough to kill off billions of human beings.

banks, saddling their customers with enormous losses.

Earlier this year, in the case of Puerto Rico, some of the world's largest banks, again including Santander and UBS, were caught red-handed while similarly off-loading bad Puerto Rican municipal bonds from their own books, while at the same time suckering their clients into buying them. And in Italy, four banks were bailed in, in December 2015 by expropriating the holdings in the banks of 10,000 of their clients. The same theft is now beginning in Portugal and other countries, with deadly consequences.

YouTube/Euronews videograb

A June 2015 rally against austerity in Greece. Southern Europeans are acutely aware of the danger the City of London-Wall Street policy means for their lives.

And now this fraudulent practice has been codified as not only fully "legal" under the new bail-in regulations implemented by the European Union as of Jan. 1, 2016, but it is furthermore being *required* of Europe's banks, to sell "bail-in bonds" (bonds that would be instantly expropriated in the case of the bank's insolvency) to the tune of 8% of their total assets. The identical policy was put on the books in the United States with the infamous Dodd-Frank bill, rammed through Congress by Barack Obama with Wall Street money.

The desperate lunacy of the bail-in scheme has many in Europe alarmed. For example, the former head of the Italian Deposit Guarantee Fund (FITD), Paolo Savona, wrote in an article for *Milano Finanza* in early January that the EU bank resolution mechanism is arbitrary, and guaranteed to fail: "The Guidelines on Resolution of banking crises has the typical features of European Treaties and regulations, which forecast everything except those cases that are really important, in case of major crises … I fought against the approved mechanism as long as I was allowed to do it by those who prefer the rule of men to the rule of laws."

Even the City of London's *Financial Times* is nervous about what they have unleashed, noting that banks that have been bailed in—such as Portugal's Novo Banco—have immediately had their credit rating reduced. That is also expected to happen with any bank that begins to actually market bail-in bonds. Furthermore, the *Financial Times* admits, smaller banks will be unable to market any bail-in bonds, and will be gob-

bled up by the already bloated mega-banks. It quotes investment banker Davide Serra saying: "This should also trigger consolidation of the smaller banks as a lot of them could be cut out of the bond market."

In fact, *no* European banks were able to market any bonds whatsoever in the first week of 2016.

The Decisive Battleground

But the decisive battleground, both on bail-in *per se* and the broader question of the blowout of the world financial system, is the United States. The $2 quadrillion financial bomb must be defused by shutting down Wall Street and declaring all its supposed assets null and void, as Lyndon LaRouche has insisted, and the way to do that is by immediately returning to FDR's Glass-Steagall law. The cowardly Congress should never have left Washington for the Christmas holiday without passing that legislation, but now that they are back in session, their feet must be held to the fire to pass Glass-Steagall as the first order of business.

The Presidential campaign has become a sounding board for the beginnings of a discussion of Glass-Steagall, but that must now become a stampede for action, while it is still possible to prevent the devastation that otherwise awaits us under the British Empire and Obama's rule. It is time to listen to the wise words of Lyndon LaRouche: "What you have to do is, pose out the fact that there will be no solution, unless Wall Street is put out of business right now. And that's what Franklin Roosevelt did in effect. He shut down Wall Street."

—Dennis Small

EIR Contents

www.larouchepub.com Volume 43, Number 3, January 15, 2016

Cover This Week

President Franklin D. Roosevelt in Mandan, North Dakota, August 27, 1936

To Break Free, Germany Needs The New Silk Road Marshall Plan!

by Helga Zepp-LaRouche, chair of the German political party Civil Rights Movement Solidarity.

Jan. 9—In the highly charged national and international debate about what happened in Cologne on New Year's Eve and about what the refugee policy should be, most people forget the context in which these developments are playing out. In the trans-Atlantic region, the financial crash is fully on, and since several countries have already implemented the 'bail-in' policy, which means the expropriation of the depositors and the creditors of insolvent banks (the "Cyprus model"), speculators shied away from buying bonds in the first week of January. Directly linked to the collapse is the growing danger of a global thermonuclear war.

Regardless of what a thorough investigation brings to light about the attacks on the women in Cologne by "North African-looking" gangs of men, these incidents are grist for the mills of right-wingers, from British Prime Minister David Cameron to Donald Trump, to the *Alternativ für Deutschland* party and all those who have attacked Chancellor Merkel's refugee policy, and hope to reduce the number of asylum seekers as much as possible. Deputy Finance Minister Jens Spahn, who has written a book strongly attacking Merkel's policy, has launched a populist call for a "social outcry."

Such an outcry is indeed necessary, not only against the barbaric culprits in Cologne, but especially against those responsible for the refugee crisis,—the Bushes, Cheneys, Obamas, Blairs, and Camerons who have blanketed South-West Asia with wars based on lies, and who have knowingly and willfully built up terrorist organizations from the Mujahideen to al-Qaeda, al-Nusra, and ISIS to bring down elected governments for geopolitical reasons, including by providing them with weapons. The "failure of the state" that Spahn decries in Merkel's refugee policy, is in reality the "failure of the policy" of the Anglo-American Empire, which has laid waste to Iraq, Afghanistan, Libya, Syria, and now Yemen, making survival impossible for the people there, who are fleeing to places where they hope to have a chance to survive.

Some Serious Questions

The police were unable to control the chaotic situation on New Year's Eve. Why there was no heightened state of alert for all main train stations, when the Munich

Investigators confirmed Monday that about a thousand inebriated men were responsible for the rampage,

http://vladtepesblog.com

German Federal Justice Minister Heiko Maas stated in a Jan. 10 Bild am Sonntag interview that the New Year's Eve Cologne riots, shown here, were "inter-coordinated or pre-planned," and that "we must urgently have intelligence on this."

and Munich-Pasing stations were closed down twice, raises a number of questions. In any case, Germany now has the "ugly images" which Spahn, in his book, believes have to be "accepted" as a result of drastic measures against the refugees. But instead of the screaming women and children being expelled, which he evokes, this time we only saw the temporarily lawless area around the Cologne main station.

Those responsible are, among others, the advocates of the "black zero" deficit policy, i.e., a monetarist austerity policy under which the debt incurred by the state to save the speculators and bankrupt banks is foisted onto the population, and investors' accounts are seized to cover current banking debts. In other words, those responsible are Finance Minister Wolfgang Schäuble and his Deputy Minister Spahn, whose policy led to the layoff of 16,000 police over the past years, just as demands on the police were increasing to ensure security at soccer games, rock concerts, and border controls. The police trade unions have repeatedly warned about the consequences of the staff downsizing.

If the mixture of hostility and social callousness shown by Schäuble and company in the case of Greece, and towards the refugees and now Italy, represents the "community of values" and "defining culture" which should allegedly make us superior, then nobody who has any humanity left at all would want to be anywhere near these people. Among these people are not only Schäuble, whom even his friends in his political party say would sell his grandmother to implement his idea of a European superstate, and Jens Spahn, whose call to "be willing to get tough" presents an extremely ugly image—the "hateful German," so to speak.

Expressing similar thinking, Schäuble's former close collaborator Markus Kerber—presently the managing director of the German Industrial Association—said in his contribution to Spahn's book that the effort to be made for the integration of the refugees, "depends on the dose." As if these desperate people needed a few drops of medicine against a cold.

Germans Must Decide

We in Germany in particular, and in the trans-Atlantic sector as a whole, are facing a total dichotomy. On one hand there are people, such as the many volunteers helping with the refugee crisis, who, in the face of the obvious crisis of civilization, are giving their all, their humanity. On the other hand there are those profiteering off the system, who, according to the principle of the

swiss-image.ch/Moritz Hager
Germany's chief budget-cutter, Federal Minister of Finance Wolfgang Schäuble, speaking in Davos, Switzerland, Jan. 24, 2014.

three monkeys who can see, hear, or say no evil, defend everything that can preserve their oh-so-comfortable privileges. They do that even if that goes hand in hand with "ugly images," such as the looming collapse into a new Dark Age, or the extinction of mankind in a third, thermonuclear world war. The principle that holds is: If the Titanic sinks, I still want to at least have the best seat at the final dinner with the Captain.

That was expressed so prophetically in Schiller's *Song of the Bell*:

> Doch mit des Geschickes Mächten
> Ist kein ew'ger Bund zu flechten,
> Und das Unglück schreitet schnell.

> But with the powers of Destiny
> No lasting bond may woven be;
> And Misfortune strideth swift.

Whoever thinks that he can build his career as a popstar of politics now by becoming an apologist for globalization—which is at the point of totally disappearing into hell,—is just a fool of the same sort that Sebastian Brant wrote about in his 1494 satire, *The Ship of Fools*.

Just as foolish is the clique of journalists which repeats the mantra that the collapse of the Chinese stock market is responsible for the crash now underway. The Chinese stock market is only a small part of the Chinese economy, and the government is now shrinking it. Meanwhile, China has overtaken Japan and South Korea in terms of the export of high technology goods, such as high-speed trains, satellites, nuclear technology, and so forth. In the midst of the currently escalating financial crash, it is the real economic capacities which survive, while virtual stock market values can be wiped out with a keystroke on the computer.

The 'Punctum Saliens'

There is currently only one strategic initiative which can provide a solution for the different crises we face—the financial, economic, refugee, and moral crises—and that is the offer by the Chinese government for cooperation in construction of a new Silk Road, on the basis of a "win-win" strategy. We must shut down the casino economy of the City of London and Wall Street, of which Schäble, Spahn, Kerber, and the prematurely ousted Asmussen are toadies, by immediately implementing a system of bank separation in the tradition of Franklin Roosevelt's Glass-Steagall law. And then we need a credit system, like the one we had with the Kreditanstalt für Wiederaufbau (Reconstruction Bank) after World War II.

The refugee crisis will not be solved by the ugly, abominable methods of Herr Spahn, nor by the just as unrealistic proposals of Wolfgang Ischinger, who also contributed to Spahn's book. The only way to do it is to develop both Southwest Asia and Africa with a comprehensive "Marshall Plan." And the only proposal that exists is the construction of the New Silk Road, as a development plan for all of Southwest Asia and Africa.

If we, in Germany, are to assume the historical responsibility which has more or less fallen into our laps, we have to take the initiative now and commit ourselves to the 'Silk Road Marshall Plan' before the possibility to act is taken out of our hands by the escalating events.

Since New Year's Eve at the latest, it should have been clear for all thinking people that we have come to an historical point which Friedrich Schiller described as the *'punctum saliens,'* or as the crucial point in the drama. Should we fail, it will lead to a tragedy, but should we seize the occasion to establish a new paradigm, we will usher in a new era for mankind. The New Silk Road, as a program to develop the destroyed and under-developed regions of the world, is the opportunity that we must now seize.

We Have No Other Agenda

Jan. 7—Our only agenda is that laid out at length by Lyndon LaRouche in a meeting with associates Tuesday evening, Jan. 6. He began by referring to his forecast that all Hell would break loose after Jan. 1, as it certainly has begun to,— but the detailed further course of the collapse is still undetermined. He went on to point to the success of the Manhattan Project— of organizing the American people around the necessity, and possibility, of choral beauty—despite all of its difficulties (see *EIR, Jan. 8, 2016*). That Manhattan Project is now the key to history; if LaRouche had not launched it as he did in October 2014, now all would be lost.

He identified that it is the British system, top down, which is driving towards a global mass killing of the human population. The British royal family is determined to reduce the human population to a small fragment of what it is today. Asia will not be destroyed by the impact of the economic collapse which is now striking the trans-Atlantic area, but precisely for that reason, the British Empire, through Obama, is determined to destroy Asia and Russia in war.

LaRouche then said:

So, therefore, our objective has to be to destroy the British Empire. If you don't destroy the British Empire, you're not going to be alive. That's what the issue is. And the issue is that most people are stupid because, out of fear, they don't want to do something like that. The only way we can save the population of the planet is to get rid of everything that is the British authority, especially the British Isles authority, British royal family and its legacy. ... and destroy the forces in the United States which were the guilty party in the incumbent Presidency of the United

If you don't destroy the British Empire, you're not going to survive. Here, British officers execute some leaders of the Indian Rebellion of 1857, by tying them to the muzzles of cannon and blowing them to pieces. They massacred thousands of noncombatants during the rebellion. Larger numbers died in famines as a result of British policy.

States, and in much of the leadership of the organization of the United States. Because you see what they are doing, they are leading the march toward the destruction of the population of the United States.

Look what's happened! Look at the death rates imposed by Obama, by Obama's policies on the people of the United States. So you're not in a situation of an economic problem *as an economic problem,* but the intention is mass murder. So saying you've got a program to solve the threat of economic problems, you're kidding yourself. The intention is, by hook or by crook, to reduce the population of the planet massively, and suddenly.

Obama, witting agent of the British Imperial policy to depopulate the United States and the world, toasts the Queen at Winfield House, London, in 2011.

And the only way you can deal with that is to beat the enemy. And that is what the Presidency and what the organization of the Congress would not do. The Congress had the authority to *shut this project down.* And they decided to go ahead. That was the decision that was made in December. The final decision at the point the Congress adjourned, was a decision *to destroy the United States.* Unless you denounce them for that, and scare the shit out of them, they're going to continue to do that.

That's what's going on in Europe. Europe is headed for a death-knell. And unless you take the action to destroy the British interests and those things that correspond to British interests, you have no means by which to avoid the kind of nightmare which is sitting there waiting to fall on us. If you get out there and say we insist we're going to get the members of Congress and punish them for what they're trying to do, you don't have anything.

In other words, there's no way you can *adapt* to this situation. If you try to adapt to it, you're just going to make a fool of yourself. You've got to throw this President out of office. And you've got to throw out the members of Congress who'll

go along with him, too. That's the only chance we have, from the standpoint of the United States. Right now, all of Western Europe is headed for the death-knell, on the basis of economic and related conditions. And the only thing you have is Asia, the Asian area, or the core of the Asian area. And therefore the British will not let that alone by any means. So you have to go out and just wipe out the royal family. Want to do that?

The Underlying Problem

LaRouche went on, at a later point in the meeting, to point to the underlying nature of the problem:

Look in particular at what you get from Abraham Lincoln's assassination, and then you put in the other things that went with it; then you see the process leading in from that. You see the same outcome from the Civil War, and that led to the next step: One decade before the end of the century, Bismarck was put out of office. The 1890s were a horror period that led immediately to general warfare. We've had perpetual warfare, despite all the talk about peace. We've had general warfare forever. So therefore, it's these guys who said, "Be practical."

What we're discussing here is the actual truth; we're taking certain elements of the absolute truth of history, and we're looking at it from the standpoint of an earlier period, as a record. We say, "Hey, this keeps going on!" and it's a threat to the entirety of humanity, it's not a series of local problems. And Obama is simply a key Satanic figure; he is an agent of the British Empire. His stepfather, of course, was part of the same thing; part of the same British kind of operation.

So, that's the problem we have; you have to recognize that *this* phenomenon is what the issue is. It's not Joe Doaks or somebody doing something, this is a phenomenon. And in certain parts of history, mankind has been able to deal with these kinds of threats. But they never stuck; they kept coming back, the same kind of phenomena.

Take the Papacy in a certain earlier period. You had a great leader who built all the water systems in Europe [Charlemagne]. He did it; and as soon as he died, Hell broke loose. And the Catholic Church became a piece of sodomy, immediately at that point. You have to know what happened when Charlemagne died; after his death, the Satanic movement took over the Catholic Church. What you got with the Renaissance was essentially again an attempt,—which is really a decade,—and then again, the same thing hit. And you see what happened after that.

You see the death of Leibniz, and that was not an intended one; even though there was an intention to have that done. But the death of Leibniz was the occasion for getting the influence of Leibniz out; and Leibniz was organizing heavily with China, he was a leading factor inside China at that time. Well, when you look at it from the standpoint of real history, it becomes clearer.

And the problem is, people don't use the right language when they refer to these events. If you put the right tag on it, you would deal with the problem. If somebody says, "Somebody in California killed some people," and you try to isolate that, then Obama gets by with that by deliberately protecting these guys [a reference to a

mass killing organized by the ISIS in southern California on Dec. 2, 2015]. They had actually instigated them, because he was part of the instigation. And people say, "Well, these guys did it. Maybe it isn't that important; maybe it was just a few people." In fact, it's not; Obama was the mother of this terror show in California. And sometimes, you know, the males can be the mother in cases like that....

All these practical explanations: "this is that," a simple explanation of this fact and that fact, which goes on in our own organization, is something that makes us impotent and self-destructive. When we have qualities of things which in a more general way,— when you get too narrow in your focus, you lose perspective. In other words, you see a fact; you say, "Well, this is a fact, and this is my fact." But it doesn't take into account the things that make those facts possible.

No, this has to be seen and handled in a certain way; because we're dealing with a population inside the United States, and most of the people in the United States are pretty stupid,—I have to admit that, for the sake of the American people and their decisions."

LaRouche's Role

At the end of the meeting, LaRouche reviewed how he had been brought into the incoming Ronald Reagan administration, before Reagan was inaugurated, by then still-functioning elements of the intelligence apparatus of Franklin Roosevelt.

LaRouche was key in organizing many of the policies of Reagan, which were the appropriate expression of Roosevelt's intentions for this period of the late 1970s and early 1980s. The response of the British Imperial enemy, of whom the Bush family are puppets, was to attempt, again, to kill a President. "They didn't kill him, but they almost killed him," LaRouche said, and during Reagan's long convalescence, George H.W. Bush, who had been forced on him as Vice President, took over. LaRouche was railroaded to prison as part of the same operation.

"So therefore, I have a certain responsibility in this matter," LaRouche said. "My responsibility is meeting the challenge of what has to be done; I'm the heir of the victim."

Jerry Brown and the Murder of California's Youth

by Robert Ingraham

Introduction

Jan. 7—As will be made clear in this report, the current state of youth culture in California represents an existential threat to the very existence of human civilization. Over a 40-year time span, the actual content of what it means to be a human being has been increasingly stripped from the minds and hearts of California youth. Mis-educated, corrupted, degraded, and discarded, California's youth are lost at sea, and no one has offered them a moral or intellectual compass to find their bearings.

As for Jerry Brown, the following discourse is not intended as an in-depth personal profile of Brown; rather, it presents a dissection of precisely how his 41-year career has destroyed the State of California, and how it has produced two generations of mentally and morally crippled youth. There is no exaggeration in stating that the overriding constant throughout Brown's career has been his continuing outright Satanic view as to the nature of the human species. This outlook was first announced by Brown during the initial days of his first round as California Governor in 1975, and he has never wavered from this anti-human outlook down to the present day.

Brown first served as Governor from 1975 to 1983, following the two preceding Governors, Ronald Reagan (1967-1975) and Brown's father, "Pat" Brown (1959-1967). Brown returned to the governorship in 2011, and has now three years more to serve of his current term. It is also critical to note that the period from 1975 to 2016 included not only 13 years of Brown as governor, but also eight years of Arnold Schwarzenegger in the State House. Thus, for 21 out of the last 41 years—the last 13 years consecutively—California has been ruled not merely by incompetents, but by representatives of pure evil.

I. Jerry Brown's Hatred of Human Beings

In November of 2015, Jerry Brown, at the personal invitation of President Barack Obama, attended the United Nations Climate Change Conference (COP21) in Paris as a member of the U.S. delegation. This con-

Justin Catanoso

Jerry Brown speaking at a side-forum at the recent Summit on Depopulation in Paris, COP21, on Dec. 6.

ference, which followed by five months the release of Pope Francis' Malthusian encyclical *Laudato Si'*, has been the most aggressive effort to date by the British Monarchy to impose a global regime of mandatory human genocide.

Although the recruitment of the Vatican to the drive for mass-murder is a new development, Brown has been obsessed with a "defense of nature" against hated human beings throughout the last 41 years. During his first go-around as Governor, Brown was a leading advocate for the Carter Administration's (1977) Global 2000 policy, the first official U.S. government policy statement that called for national population reduction. In 1978, Brown appointed Huey Johnson as Director of Resources for the State of California. During that period, Johnson delivered a speech at the National Press Club, calling on California to adopt a population limitation policy, including tax penalties for large families, immigration restrictions, abortion legislation, and curtailment of low-income housing.

Between 1975 and 1983 Brown appointed a whole gaggle of pro-drug, pro-green freaks to leading positions in the California government, including Gregory Bateson, the husband of Margaret Mead, and Willis Harman from the Stanford Research Institute, both of whom were appointed to the Board of Regents of the University of California. Bateson, a British national, began his career as a student of Norbert Wiener's work in cybernetics, and developed his own theories claiming that schizophrenia and other mental aberrations were all the product of chemical and other physical-mechanical imbalances in the human brain, which could be corrected through the use of psychotropic drugs.

Bateson was also for many years on intimate terms with both counterculture gurus Aldous Huxley and Alan Watts. And in 1959 he was appointed Director of the MK-ULTRA LSD experiment at the Palo Alto Veterans Hospital, where Ken Kesey and others who would carry out the 1965-1966 "acid tests" in California were recruited to the drug culture.

One of the individuals who played a leading role with Bateson and Kesey, in the creation of the LSD-movement was Stewart Brand. In 1977 Jerry Brown appointed Brand as his "special advisor," and from that position Brand played a leading role in promoting a green fascist agenda, including his advocacy of solar energy and his leading role in both successfully killing

the proposed Sun Desert nuclear plant, and attempting to shut down the Diablo Canyon nuclear plant. Brand, with Brown's backing, also endorsed a farm acreage policy to limit federal water consumption by state farmers.

'Under 2 MOU'

In May of 2015, a new pro-genocide organization was created, based on an initial agreement between the State of California and the German State of Baden Württemberg. This organization is named "Under 2 MOU,"[1] and at its founding press conference, representatives of 12 local and regional governments—including California, Baden Württemberg, Vermont, Oregon, Ontario, British Columbia, Catalonia, Wales, and Baja California—released a statement which committed their local governments to a policy of reducing "greenhouse gas emissions" (including CO_2) to a level of 80% to 95% below 1990 levels by 2050.

From the beginning, Jerry Brown has been the initiator and leading organizer of Under 2 MOU. Working in conjunction with Papal advisor Hans Joachim Schellnhuber[2] of the Pontifical Academy of Sciences, Brown was able to elevate Under 2 MOU to a leading role at the COP21 Paris conference. On Dec. 5, 2015, during the Paris Conference, Brown held a press conference announcing 43 new signatories to the Under 2 Mou agreement, bringing the total number of signers to 123 separate jurisdictions. A partial list includes: the cities of New York, Vancouver, Seattle, Austin, San Francisco, Oakland, and Los Angeles; the states of New Hampshire, New York, Connecticut, Minnesota, Rhode Island, and Washington; numerous cities and provinces from Britain, France, Germany, the Netherlands, Portugal, Italy, Spain, Brazil, Mexico, China, Japan, and Canada; and other governments from Africa and South America.[3]

Although several sovereign nations have signed on to Under 2 MOU, the primary role of the organization is to bypass national governments, going directly to state and local agencies, for the purpose of implementing

---

1. MOU is an acronym for "Memorandum Of Understanding."
2. The knighted Schellnhuber is notorious for demanding the reduction of the world's population to below one billion people, in complete agreement with the repeated statements of Britain's Prince Philip.
3. Brown was accompanied to Paris by Arnold Schwarzenegger, who heads up his own pro-genocide organization known as Regions of Climate Action (The R20).

Anthropologist Gregory Bateson, with his wife Margaret Mead, at work in Papua, New Guinea in 1938.

genocide on a state and regional scale, and then pressuring national governments into acquiescing to the Malthusian demands of COP21. At his Paris press conference announcing the newest members of Under 2 MOU, Jerry Brown stated, "The real source of climate action has to come from states and provinces. We're going to build up such a drumbeat that our national counterparts—they're going to listen ... after Paris, the real work begins."

Brown is not waiting for others to act. In 2015, Brown signed an Executive Order which requires California to cut greenhouse gas emissions 40% below 1990 levels by 2030—the most ambitious target in North America. Brown announced that utilities would have to get 50% of their energy from "renewable" sources by 2030, and that California would seek to double efficiency savings from existing buildings. Industries will have to cut smokestack releases, and electric cars will have to become affordable enough to capture a huge portion of the market. Thankfully, even the usually supine and mentally-challenged California Legislature had the sense to defeat a bill that would have written Brown's pledges into law. Brown has threatened to ignore the legislature and use the powers of the California Air Resources Board to implement the policy changes anyway.

Brown has made no effort to hide his commitment to population reduction, which is at the heart of his recent activities. Repeatedly and publicly blaming the current California drought on "man-made global warming," Brown, in a speech before the Board of the Metropolitan Water District of Southern California last June, stated, "It's a very catastrophic existential threat that we have to take as seriously as though we were facing a military adversary.... We have wreaked havoc on our natural resources, including the water systems of this state.... At some point, how many people can we accommodate?"

In May of 2015, when Brown announced a mandatory 25% cut in statewide water consumption, he stated: "For over 10,000 years, people lived in California, but the number of those people were never more than 300,000 or 400,000. Now we are embarked upon an experiment that no one has ever tried: 38 million people, with 32 million vehicles, living at the level of comfort that we all strive to attain. This will require adjustment." Compare Brown's sentiments to the words of the royal mad-man Prince Philip, who has avowed, "You cannot keep a bigger flock of sheep than you are capable of feeding. In other words, conservation may involve culling in order to keep a balance between the relative numbers in each species within any particular habitat. I realize this a very touchy subject, but the fact remains that mankind is part of the living world."[4]

The Demon Speaks

Lest one think that the charges leveled against Brown in the above section are exaggerated, it is necessary to go beyond Brown's "official" policy statements, and to examine Brown's personal beliefs. These are best gleaned from a series of informal one-on-one discussions which took place during the 1990s. From 1994 to 1998, during a period when he did not hold elective office, Jerry Brown hosted an Oakland-based syndicated radio show, titled "We the People." The show consisted primarily of a series of interviews with his personally selected guests, almost all of whom represented "alternative" views.

---

4. *The Genocidal Roots of Bush's 'New World Order'*, *EIR* Special Report, May 1992. The need for the 'culling' of the human 'herd' permeates Prince Philip's interviews, writings, and speeches. As an example, see his book *Down to Earth*, The Stephen Greene Press, Lexington, Massachusetts, 1988.

Among those hosted by Brown were the eco-feminist and anti-development NGO agitator Vandana Shiva, author of *The Plunder of Nature*; the de-schooler Ivan Illich; the eco-terrorist Judi Bari; the beatnik poet Gary Snyder; Noam Chomsky; Susannah Sheffer, editor of the magazine *Growing Without Schooling*; David Korten, author of *The Mythologies of Global Development*; and Wolfgang Sachs, author of *The Design of a Sustainable Future*. A hand-picked selection of these discussions was published in 1998 under the title **Dialogues**.

Taken as a whole, these dialogues represent a massive attack on modern science, modern agriculture, and advanced human culture. Human civilization, including specifically human population growth, is attacked repeatedly both by Brown and his guests. A continuing theme throughout the interviews is the sacredness of "nature," the destructiveness of human society, and the demand that mankind must find a "sustainable" co-relationship with Mother Earth.

In the interview with Vandana Shiva, a major focus of the discussion is an attack on the Indian Green Revolution (of modern agricultural methods and hybrid crops), and a demand to return to historical "indigenous" farming methods. Such an approach would require a drastic slashing of the human population.

In the interview with Ivan Illich, the Maoist Cultural Revolution in China is held up for praise, particularly the forced relocation of scientists and intellectuals into the countryside to engage in manual labor. In the interview with Gary Snyder, both Brown and Snyder engage in a lengthy attack on modern science and industrial civilization. At one point in the discussion, Brown states, "The Holocaust (against the Jews) was not a product of civilization gone off the track; it was an extension of civilization, which, by definition, socializes individuals against their own state of nature, their true nature."

Ivan Illich (1926-2002), leader of the deschooling movement internationally.

II. The Destruction of California

It may come as a surprise to many people who associate California with Hollywood and surfing, that between 1940 and 2000 California was the leading state in the nation in both agriculture and industry, and that during that same period revenues from both agribusiness and the aerospace industry outstripped those of the Hollywood film "industry" by a very large margin.

Beginning in 1975, Jerry Brown announced that the pro-growth era of his father, the FDR-Democrat Pat Brown,[5] was now over, that California had now entered an "era of limits." Over the next eight years, Brown unleashed an all-out assault against the advanced scientific-industrial heritage of California. This included attacks on California agriculture, the aerospace industry, and the nuclear power industry.

Earlier, Pat Brown had been a champion of nuclear power in California. It was during his governorship that the first nuclear power plant opened in the state. Later, under Governor Ronald Reagan in 1970, California adopted a Master Plan for the construction of eleven new nuclear plant sites, each site to contain multiple reactors, projected to increase the percentage of nuclear power-generated electricity from 2% to 50% by 1990. Once he took office in 1975, Jerry Brown scrapped all of these plans. No new plants were built, and Brown did everything he could to close the existing plants.

Water & Agriculture

As a result of the efforts of Franklin Roosevelt and Pat Brown, today California produces more than half of all of the fresh produce in the United States, including

---

5. The California Water Project, built by Governor Pat Brown, is the largest infrastructure project undertaken and completed by an individual state in American history.

84% of the country's fresh peaches, 94% of the country's fresh plums, 99% of the artichokes, 94% of the broccoli, and 94% of the tomatoes.

In response to the ongoing drought in California, last May Brown ordered a 25% cut in the state's water consumption, with the brunt of this to be borne by California farmers. Thousands of farmers simply found it impossible to obtain fresh water for irrigation, and this was on top of previous water cuts to farmers during the preceding five years. By the end of 2014, 500,000 acres of farmland lay fallow in California, costing the state's agriculture industry $1.5 billion in revenue and 17,000 jobs. The figures are not yet in for 2015, but most experts believe the total acreage of fallowed farmland for 2015 could double.

There has already been a 20% decline in the rice crop, and a 35% drop in the cotton crop, both of which are the largest in the nation. Anyone driving down Interstate 5 recently has witnessed the sight of mile after mile of dead almond and peach orchards, killed by a lack of water.

Throughout all of this, Brown has squashed any proposals for developing new water resources, including desalinization facilities or new reservoirs. Instead, as he stated to one reporter, his view is that "It's a different world. We have to think differently. The idea of... getting lots of water every day, that's going to be a thing of the past."

Aerospace

It is estimated that in 1990, the aerospace industry accounted for 1.4 million direct and indirect jobs in California. Today this is down to about 500,000 jobs

The sleep of reason produces monsters, by Francisco Goya, no. 43 of his Los Caprichos, 1799. Goya's caption reads: "Imagination abandoned by reason produces impossible monsters: united with her, she is the mother of the arts and the source of their wonders."

(200,000 directly and 300,000 in supporting industries), a decline of 65%.

Not only is aerospace California's largest industry; with an average annual pay of $81,536, aerospace manufacturing jobs pay 50% more than other typical manufacturing positions, and dramatically more than the minimum wage and other low-wage service sector jobs which are proliferating across the state. Additionally, the majority of the aerospace jobs that have been lost have been in Los Angeles County, leaving that area economically and culturally more and more at the mercy of Hollywood.

In 1960, 15 of the largest 25 aerospace companies in the United States were based in southern California. Despite cutbacks during the 1970s and 1980s, even as late as 1987, California accounted for one in four aerospace jobs nationally. Today, all but a handful of these firms have closed their doors.

This out-and-out destruction of California's aerospace industry has escalated since the year 2000, during the administrations of the Hollywood actor Arnold Schwarzenegger and the anti-industry Jerry Brown. And this collapse is continuing to date. In 2015, the massive Boeing Long Beach plant, where the C-17 military cargo planes were built, closed permanently. Governor Brown made no attempt to keep the facility open.

While the skilled workforce and the advanced industry of California has been decimated, television filming in Los Angeles County increased 12% from 2013 to 2014; and in September 2014 Governor Brown signed a bill increasing the state's annual subsidy of the film industry from $110 million to $330 million.

III. Education

There is a great misunderstanding in the ongoing discussion of education in the United States. Often this comes in the form of ranking states in terms of how much money they are spending on education, or what the results from standardized tests show.

But there is a yardstick of far, far greater importance. What of developing the creative potentials of the students? Not un-rigorous artsy-fartsy masturbation mis-named as creativity, but the actual scientific creative potential of their minds. The study of Classical music, the study of great scientific breakthroughs from the past, the understanding of how human civilization has progressed over the recent millennia. What is actually being done in the schools today to prepare young students to develop into productive, creative citizens in the Twenty-first Century, to contribute to the future betterment of humanity?

Before turning to the heart of the matter, it should be said that dollars and cents are not unimportant, and, it must be noted that between 1975 and 1983, during Brown's first tenure as Governor, California dropped from fifth to forty-fifth place nationally in the funding of schools as a percentage of the total personal income of the people of the state. Apologists for Jerry Brown blame this collapse on Proposition 13,[6] but it should be remembered that Brown enthusiastically endorsed Prop 13, signed it into law, and when he ran for re-election, he was strongly backed by Prop 13's author, the virulent "tax crusader" and budget cutter, Howard Jarvis.

Might not the pupil know more? Caprichos no. 37, which Goya captions: "One cannot say whether he knows more or less; what is certain is that the master is the most serious-looking person who could possibly be found."

Today, California ranks at or near the bottom on almost all facets of primary and secondary education. For example, California ranks last in the nation as it has the worst ratio of number of students per teacher. The national average is 15.9 students per teacher; in California it is 24.9. In terms of class size, California ranks forty-ninth for elementary schools and fiftieth for secondary schools, with the average class size for both being about 30 students. This has worsened since Brown began his second tenure as Governor in 2011. In 1965, California ranked fifth in the nation in per-pupil spending. By 2012 it ranked forty-third.

Destroying Young Minds

Lyndon LaRouche has repeatedly denounced the influence of John Dewey over U.S. educational policy during the Twentieth Century. And although Dewey's influence is a national phenomenon, nowhere were his methods more fully put into practice than in California.

This, of course, did not start with Jerry Brown. The Dewey educational approach was widespread in California beginning in the 1930s and 1940s. By 1950 it was hegemonic in a way which probably existed nowhere else in the United States. It came under attack during the Cold War years, but returned with a vengeance during the "counterculture" years of the 1960s and 1970s. Although, on the surface, the methods of Dewey were seemingly overturned with a return to basics, and the "standardized testing" brought in by George Bush's 2001 "No Child Left Behind" legislation, this is actually far from the truth. The core of the Deweyite approach remains dominant to this day.

John Dewey is famous for his many writings on

---

6. The California ballot initiative which cut local property taxes, and thus led to the reduction of funding for the schools.

education, including *The School and Society* (1899), *The Child and the Curriculum* (1902), *Moral Principles in Education* (1909), *How We Think* (1910), and *Democracy and Education: An Introduction to the Philosophy of Education* (1916). What is less well known is that prior to writing one word on education, in 1888, Dewey authored a work titled *Leibniz's New Essays Concerning the Human Understanding: a Critical Exposition*. In this rather lengthy work, Dewey offers faint praise to Gottfried Leibniz, but then proceeds to attack all of Leibniz' key conceptions, including the notion of "sufficient reason," and Leibniz's views on God, the Monad, and human creativity. He praises Kant as the person who corrected Leibniz's errors. In particular, he takes great pains to disprove a relationship between the Monad and the Universal, thus denying any link between the individual human mind and the principle of Universal Creativity.

These core beliefs of Dewey's—that true human creativity does not exist, that universal truths are unknowable and probably non-existent, and that all learning is acquired through sense experience—are the axiomatic bedrock of all of his teachings. Everything which is draped over those key axioms, all of the trappings about the role of the teacher, attending to the physical needs of the students, promoting democracy and social consciousness—these are simply elaborations of his essential philosophy. And rather than get caught up in the mere facets of so-called "progressive education," it is essential to return again and again to the reality of Dewey's bestial view of humanity to be able to grasp the catastrophic damage his influence has produced.

There are many things written about Dewey's educational approach, both pro and con, but almost all of these writings deal with the *structural form* taken by some of his methods, e.g., the relationship between teacher and student, or the emphasis on learning-by-doing. What they all ignore is that the key to Dewey's approach is in his concept of the human mind as he defines it in his critique of Leibniz. For Dewey, truth does not exist. Human intellect exists, but it is incapable of penetrating into the causality of universal principles. The world can only be perceived through experience, and learning consists of a succession of such sensory experiences.

Dewey's philosophy came to be known as *pragmatism*, or sometimes as *instrumentalism*, due to the emphasis it placed on practical experience, as opposed to

Library of Congress

Education destroyer John Dewey (1859-1952).

higher truths. For Dewey, the mind is conceived in purely mechanical terms. What is the mind? A tool for coping with the environment. What is "true?" Whatever is practical, whatever works within the environment.

In 1896, Dewey opened his own school, The Laboratory School, at the University of Chicago. This allowed him to put his theories into practice. The first thing to be jettisoned was the traditional approach to "Classical" education. No Classical music, no Cicero, no Aeschylus, no Shakespeare. Scholastic work was replaced with learning by doing. Truth, to the extent there is any truth at all, can only be learned through sense observation and experience. Teachers became guides; their role was not to teach but rather to guide the students to self-learn through their own experience. A high importance was placed on group learning and the development of socialization and group democracy.

Particularly condemned by Dewey was any notion of an "inner personality." Students were criticized for wanting to study or reflect on their own; instead, they were strongly encouraged to socialize all of their learning with the larger group, and to submit to the democratic consensus of the group. Dewey was obsessed with the idea of democracy, but in practice, this became the democracy of the herd, and Dewey was explicit about using education to mold the beliefs and outlooks of the students. Dissent was not encouraged.

In 1917, Dewey left Chicago and helped to found the Lincoln School of Teachers College at Columbia University in New York City, "as a laboratory for the working out of an elementary and secondary curriculum which shall eliminate obsolete material and endeavor to work up in usable form material adapted to the needs of modern living." Teachers College itself became a branch of Columbia University, while the subsumed Lincoln School developed as a separate laboratory school for children, modeled on, but going beyond, Dewey's previous effort in Chicago. To this day, Teachers College remains both a bastion of Dewey's influence as well as the leading institution of "educational theory" in the United States.

Beginning as early as 1920, several individuals who were trained by Dewey and his protégé William Kilpatrick at Teachers College began to operate in the State of California. With the publication by the state government of the *Teacher's Guide to Child Development* in 1930, Dewey's methods became hegemonic in California.[7]

On the surface, one might say that, during the ensuing decades, education in California was "dumbed down" in order to make it more "democratic," but that would be a simplistic and ultimately erroneous description of what happened. More accurate would be to say that education became *pluralistic,* i.e., that neither scientific truth nor human progress were henceforth included in the educational experience. The student was presented with a series of life experiences, from which they were to draw their own conclusions. If there were "facts" "to learn" in order to pass tests, those so-called facts were to be memorized, with no thought given to their ultimate truthfulness or relevance.

During the Cold War years, Dewey's methods came under attack, particularly after the 1957 launching of Sputnik by the Soviet Union. Nevertheless, they returned with a vengeance in the '60s and '70s through

the Free School Movement of Ivan Illich, Paul Goodman, and A.S. Neill. Best described as "Deweyism on hallucinogens," this movement was quickly discredited but lives on today in dozens of Charter and "experimental" schools. It is this neo-Deweyism from the 1960s of which Jerry Brown has been an adherent throughout his career, and which he has promulgated during both of his tenures as governor.

Supposedly to correct the decades-long damage created by Dewey's methods, in 2002 President George W. Bush signed into law the No Child Left Behind Act, federal legislation which mandated nationwide standardized testing, teacher and school board accountability, and mandatory levels of graduation and passing grades, among other things. In 2015, Barack Obama signed the Every Student Succeeds Act which replaced the Bush legislation. Passed with much fanfare, the Obama bill actually leaves in place almost the entirety of the "standardized testing" approach of the Bush Administration, with the one major change: that the enforcement of the intent of the legislation has now been handed over to the states. During the Civil Rights Movement of the 1960s, the Federal Government assumed more direct control over the nation's schools, precisely because of the failure of many states to even minimally educate their students. Obama's Every Student Succeeds Act has now returned the nation's educational system to the pre-Civil Rights era status of control by the states.

Although the Deweyite content of education may have been terrible, the LBJ-directed imposition of national oversight over the nation's schools was both necessary and in accordance with the 14th Amendment. It is in the interest of sovereign national government to ensure that all children have access to an excellent education. The more specific point is that, other than turning more control of the schools back to the states, Obama's legislation leaves in place the entire approach of the Bush No Child Left Behind policy. Now Jerry Brown will have more control over California's educational system, and if states, faced with massive budgetary problems, decide to slash educational spending, they will be free to do so.

So where does all this leave us? In truth, U.S. educational policy is now the worst of both worlds. The anti-human pragmatism of John Dewey still reigns supreme as the guiding philosophy of education. Even worse, Dewey's intention to use education to mold the social and moral outlooks of young students has been fully

---

7. *Democracy and Schooling in California*, by Kathleen Weiler, Palgrave MacMillan, New York, N.Y., 2011

realized, as students are now routinely taught to hate scientific progress, to accept false theories like man-made global warming as self-evident truths and to be "non-judgmental" to the point of accepting any form of polymorphous perversity as normal.

On top of this witches' brew has been grafted the standardized testing of Barack Obama and George W. Bush. The way in which this was described by one graduate of a California high school is that, "for most of the semester we were allowed to do pretty much what we wanted to do. Then for two weeks the teachers helped us cram for the exams." It is a testament to the universal quality of the human mind that any student today survives a California education with even part of his mind or morality intact.

Pretty teacher! Capricho no. 68, which Goya captions: "The broom is one of the most necessary implements for witches; for besides being great sweepers, as the stories tell, they may be able to change the broom into a fast mule and go with it where the Devil cannot reach them."

pline. Cooperation rather than competition was emphasized. To teach the benefits of "democracy," the school was run on democratic lines. Based on her experiences at the school, in 1932 Dora Russell published her own book on education, *In Defence of Children.*

There are definite differences between Russell and Dewey. Throughout his life, Russell continually belittled Dewey's pragmatic philosophy, and the Beacon Hill School provided more actual scholastic instruction than anything Dewey established, primarily because Russell was concerned with the necessity to produce the next generation of the British aristocracy. In their denial of scientific truth, human progress, and creativity, however, the two men are identical. Both share the same bestial view of the human species.

Dewey and Russell

Bertrand Russell's influence over education is less apparent than that of Dewey, but given the emphasis that Lyndon LaRouche has placed on the paramount destructive role of Russell in the Twentieth Century, it should not be passed over.

Russell was 13 years younger than Dewey, and he did not release his first book on education until 1926, when he published *On Education, Especially in Early Childhood.* This was followed with *Education and the Good Life* in 1927, and *Education and the Social Order* in 1932. In 1927, Russell and his wife Dora opened their own experimental school for children, the Beacon Hill School in West Sussex, England.

The Beacon Hill School was based on the idea that children should not be forced to follow a strictly academic curriculum. The school was run on the principle that freedom would result in maturity and self disci-

California Case Studies

In preparing this article, the author has had the opportunity to interview more than a dozen individuals who graduated from public school in California. The earliest of these was someone who graduated from high school in 1962; the most recent was an individual who graduated in 2011, so this is almost a 50 year chronology. In addition several parents who currently have children in either middle or high school were interviewed, bringing the survey down to the present day.

The first thing to report is that it was already bad in 1962. A man who attended school through ninth grade in New York City, and then moved to California, reported that the most striking difference in California was the lack of discipline. "Skipping" school was common, and drug use was far more prevalent. He also reported that in his poor New York school district he was able to play the cello in the school orchestra, where Classical pieces were performed, but in the affluent California high school to which he transferred, there was only a school band and no Classical music.

Another individual, this time a teacher at a California high school in the 1960s, reported that drug use by his students was so prevalent that he went to the principal and complained, "I can't teach these kids. They are all stoned." He was told, "Get used to it."

A woman who graduated from high school in 1969 reported her high school education to be "acceptable," but that when she then went to the State University, she was inundated with propaganda from her professors that human beings are destroying the environment. She stated that her high school education included Shakespeare and Dickens, but that when her son went to school in 1990, Shakespeare had been replaced by modern existentialist novels, that the science curriculum was worse and largely environmentalist; and that her son and many other students were constantly being pressured by the school to seek more psychological counseling. At one point her son was even subjected to an experimental program to teach young students to read without learning the alphabet.

A now middle-aged man who graduated from high school in 1980 stated that his elementary education was uneventful, but that his middle school was definitely "Deweyite." "Everyone was free to come and go as they pleased, and everybody passed." He reported widespread use of marijuana in middle school (even more in high school), as well as a significant number of students forced into Ritalin use by school authorities, with the pressured consent of the parents. Music was

Bravo! Capricho no. 38, which Goya captions: "If ears were all that were needed to appreciate it, no one could listen more intelligently; but it is to be feared that he is applauding what is soundless."

available, but the band played mostly works by Irving Berlin and Johann Strauss, Jr.

The majority of those spoken with for the purpose of this report graduated from high school after the year 2000, and it is here that the true horror of the Schwarzenegger-Brown governorships becomes apparent. Some of those interviewed attended affluent, even premier schools; others came from lower income areas.

In none of these schools (middle and high schools) was music a required course. Several students reported that orchestra, band, and choral music did not even exist in their schools, even as an extra-curricular activity. Ritalin use occurred in every school, and one woman reported that every student who started as a Ritalin user moved on to the use of ecstasy (MDMA). Widespread marijuana use was reported from every middle school (11- and 12-year-olds), with most individuals putting marijuana use at over 50% of the student body by high school. Many students came to school stoned, and drug dealing in the schools was common.

One or two respondents from low-income high schools reported horror stories of violence, gang activity, and high drop-out rates.

As to the curriculum, a few students at high-income or special charter schools read Shakespeare or other Classics. Most did not. Rabid environmentalism was taught in every instance. One student took part in a class trip to a nuclear power plant, and she and the other students were prepped by the teachers to make accusations to the plant officials about the dangers of nuclear power. Another student reports her class watching a documentary about the dangers of nuclear power in science class. Another young woman, who insisted that she herself had received a "good" education, reported that her 10- and 13-year-old nieces are today being taught extreme environmentalism, and that this began as early as first grade.

One woman described a class outing where her elementary class was taken by teachers to sleep on the beach so as to experience "life like the Native Americans." The freezing and miserable students had to be rescued in the middle of the night by their parents.

Sex education was, of course, available to all of these students, and in September of 2015 Jerry Brown signed into law AB329, making sex-ed mandatory for grades 7 through 12, the first state in the nation to do so. This new California sex education law mandates that "alternative" sexual practices must be taught as part of the required curriculum, including that "gay, lesbian, bi-sexual, and trans-gender activities must be affirmatively recognized as different sexual orientations, and that when discussing or providing examples of relationships and couples, shall be inclusive of same sex relationships." This is now part of the California school curriculum.

The horror stories just pile up: the works of America-hater Howard Zinn mandated as required reading in U.S. history class; novels such as *Lord of the Flies* are required reading for middle-schoolers; history classes which contain reams of information about genocide against the Indians, but not a word about Alexander Hamilton; science classes with lectures on global warming. Almost none of the students were taught punctuation or how to spell, with the explanation that this would stifle their creativity. One student reports that his class was instructed in "creative spelling," i.e., to spell as they wished.

Nanny's boy, Capricho no. 4, which Goya captions: "Negligence, tolerance and spoiling make children capricious, naughty, vain, greedy, lazy and insufferable. They grow up and yet remain childish. Thus is nanny's little boy."

This lunacy was aggravated in many of the schools by implementing a policy of building up the students' "self esteem." The "self esteem" movement, which was dreamed up at the Esalen Institute, became at one point fairly widespread, and its effects linger to this day.

Nothing negative was ever to be uttered to any student; bad habits or behavior were never to be corrected. Several individuals report that this approach was rampant in their schools; others claimed ignorance of it, but it is likely that they have not yet fully recognized what they were subjected to. One student reports that her teachers were not even allowed to use a red pen to correct mistakes, lest it negatively affect the pupil's morale. She also reported that when she told her teacher she wanted to sit on the floor for a class, the teacher answered, "go right ahead."

Then, in 2001 and 2002, the standardized tests of the No Child Left Behind legislation arrived in the schools. Every person spoken with who went through that transition described it as nearly insane, with teachers drilling students in the correct answers for multiple choice tests. Often, the material related to the tests was not even taught. Rather, the *answers* to the most likely list of questions were presented to the students to be memorized.

Obviously, not all schools are as bad as what is reported above. The heroic efforts of some truly caring teachers must also be noted. Nevertheless, the people interviewed were chosen at random, from schools in areas as far apart as San Diego and Sacramento. The evidence of the crime that has been perpetrated is very, very clear.

IV. Californication

If the above description of the mental and moral murder of California's youth has upset you, get prepared, for there is worse still to come.

In his novel *Brave New World*, the LSD enthusiast Aldous Huxley states that the role of the state is to bring about a condition of "Universal Happiness." For the British Empire's Huxley, however, his proposed notion of happiness bears no resemblance to the philosophical *principle* of happiness defined by Gottfried Leibniz, which is enshrined in the U.S. Declaration of Independence.

Speaking before a Google-sponsored conference in 2010, British Prime Minister David Cameron announced that the primary goal of his government was henceforth to increase the "happiness" of the British people.[8] Following this speech, Cameron implemented a policy of conducting national surveys to measure the happiness and "well-being" of the British people. Sample questions from the most recent official well-being survey include:

• How satisfied are you with your life nowadays?
• How happy did you feel yesterday?
• How anxious did you feel yesterday?
• To what extent do you feel the things you do in your life are worthwhile?

In *Brave New World*, Huxley has his own prescription for happiness. This includes:

• to abolish family life, so as to allow full sexual freedom.
• to legalize euthanasia, so as to remove the burden of dealing with the sick and elderly.
• to reduce the human population, so as to make the quality of life better for those who remain.
• to legalize drugs, so as to remove anxiety and suppress malicious bad tempers.

In a well-known quote from a 1962 lecture, Huxley said:

> There will be, in the next generation or so, a pharmacological method of making people love their servitude, and producing dictatorship without tears, so to speak, producing a kind of painless concentration camp for entire societies, so that people will in fact have their liberties taken away from them, but will rather enjoy it, because

creative commons/Christopher Michel
Degeneracy on display at the yearly, drug-sodden Burning Man festival in the Nevada desert in 2015.

they will be distracted from any desire to rebel by propaganda or brainwashing, or brainwashing enhanced by pharmacological methods. And this seems to be the final revolution.[9]

Huxley named the drug that would self-enslave the population *soma*. Today, there is not one drug, but a cornucopia of legal and illegal drugs available to anyone, to produce the "happiness" which Huxley and Cameron proclaim.

In 2015, deaths from drug abuse in California were the leading cause of death, higher than cancer, heart attacks, murder, or accidents. California has the largest "medical marijuana" market in the United States, by a very wide margin. In recent years, when federal law enforcement agencies have attempted to move against either the marijuana clinics or growers, they have often been aggressively opposed by local elected officials.

8. Getting rid of the Queen and all her blood relations might be a start.

9. From a lecture entitled ``The Ultimate Revolution,'' delivered on March 20, 1962 at the Berkeley Language Center, Berkeley, Calif.

In California today 10% of high school boys are on Ritalin;[10] 23% of women, aged 40 to 60, are on anti-depressants;[11] 13% of the population uses opioids (heroin, oxycontin, etc.); the use of ecstasy and other designer drugs are rampant in the youth culture; meth-amphetamine use is widespread, particularly among poor whites and Mexicans; and it is anybody's guess what the level of marijuana use is. California is the largest marijuana producer in the United States, so that should give some indication of the problem.

In 2014, the voters of California passed Proposition 47, a measure which reduced the penalty for drug possession (all drugs, including heroin, etc.) for personal use from a felony to a misdemeanor, the first state in the nation to do so.

In October of 2015, Jerry Brown also signed California's first Right-to-Die law, thus legalizing euthanasia and fulfilling another of Huxley's requirements for human happiness.[12]

How is your anxiety? How is your Well-Being? Is it improving?

Music, Pornography, Gaming, Mob Democracy

It is frequently stated that youth, since the 1990s, have been the first generation to grow up "on the Internet." However, they also have achieved another first. They are also the first generation to grow up with access to hard core pornography on-demand 24 hours a day.

Pornographic movies were not legalized in the United States until 1969. Prior to that they were simply unavailable to the average American. Even during the '70s and '80s, the exposure of Americans to pornographic film was very limited. Most "porno" theaters were located in urban areas. Most were "seedy" and not heavily frequented, so even if the use of pornography spread, it was still nowhere near a universal phenomenon. That all changed with the Internet.

Today, 11-, 12-, 13-year-old children (and younger) can watch pornographic movies for free, any time of the day or night. All it takes is a few clicks of a mouse. By

the time most 17-year-olds graduate from high school, to describe them as sexually "jaded" would be an understatement. The phenomenon of "sexting" is simply one small indication of the situation which now exists. This is now considered simply part of "growing up." The pornography industry itself is based in Los Angeles County, with the largest producers, including Vivid Entertainment, Wicked Pictures, and Digital Playground all operating in the San Fernando Valley.

California was also the nexus of the drug-laced rave movement during the last 20 years. Recently, raves have given way to what are called Electronic Dance Music events, many still operating in rave-type locations, but there are others which have become among the largest "entertainment" events in the world. These include California's Coachella Valley Music & Arts Festival, which in 2013 had ticket sales of over $85 million, and an attendance topping one-quarter million people. Then there is the annual celebration of nihilism known as the Burning Man Festival, which originated in San Francisco in 1986, before moving to the Nevada desert in the 1990s.

During the last 25 years, the leaders of Silicon Valley, together with their co-thinkers in Japan and elsewhere, have also brought to the youth of America the gift of digitalized video games. The "gaming industry" now accounts for over $30 *billion* a year in revenues, up from $9 billion in 2007. From the seemingly innocuous, like Candy Crush, to the point-and-shoot games emulated by many of the perpetrators of school massacres across America, millions of 15-, 25-, and 35-year-olds are literally spending *tens of millions of hours...* playing games(!), something that would have been inconceivable even one or two generations ago.

This is all Deweyite "democracy." Throw in the millions of hours that youth spend on social media, and what you see is massive pressure to conform to the accepted pleasure-seeking axioms of their peers and to the "democratic" consensus of the mob. "We are all trying to be nice people." "We are all accepting and non-discriminatory." "We all agree that human beings should stop destroying Mother Earth." Individuality is limited to what color you dye your hair, or what tattoo you get. Individual creative thinking is not even recognized to exist. There is no past worth studying and certainly no future to build.

How is your anxiety? How is your well-being? Is it improving?

---

10. Ritalin is a Schedule II psychostimulant drug used massively in the United States and Britain on children judged to have ADHD (Attention Deficit Hyperactivity Disorder). The U.S. FDA classification system includes such dangerous drugs as oxycontin and morphine as Schedule II.

11. Overall, anti-depressant usage is up 500% since 1995.

12. In signing the law, Jerry Brown stated that he was thrilled, since at some future date he might desire to kill himself.

Bon voyage, Capricho no. 64, which Goya captions: "Where is this infernal company going, filling the air with noise in the darkness of night? If it were daytime it would be quite a different matter and gun shots would bring the whole group of them to the ground; but as it is night, no one can see them."

V. Conclusion

It is a very sorry picture. And it is one that won't go away through wishful thinking. It is a massively pessimistic youth culture of conformity and other-directedness. Any real understanding of actual human history is non-existent. The culture and the schools work overtime to snuff out any individual expression of critical thinking at a very young age. It is most definitely a culture which engenders cowardice.

So what can be done? To answer that question, I would direct readers to the appendix accompanying this article which contains remarks by Lyndon LaRouche to a recent Manhattan Town Hall Meeting. The key to the solution lies there.

There are no "practical" solutions. Make no mistake; this is a war. The actual nature of human history and what it means to be a human being must be asserted and boldly defended. The evil of what Jerry Brown represents must be rubbed in the faces of both elected officials and the citizenry in general.

At the same time, in concluding this report, it must also be stated that there is no "California" solution to this catastrophe. Jerry Brown was personally invited to attend the genocidal COP21 conference in Paris by Barack Obama, the same Obama who, every Tuesday, picks the names of human beings to murder with drone attacks, the same Obama who is leading the world to World War III. This is a national fight. The lever to win it resides in the Manhattan Project of Lyndon LaRouche. Take heart! A true awakening of the human spirit can accomplish great things.

Material for this article was provided by Brian Lantz, Michael Billington, and numerous graduates from the California public school system.

Lyndon LaRouche: Educating Children For the Future

The following excerpts are from the Dec. 29, 2015 Town Hall Meeting with Lyndon LaRouche in New York City.

Question: Long story short: In my evaluating things from over the last 50 years in travel, seeing different cultures, measuring what I've learned from their interactions, the only basic thing that I see to achieve anything directly, to have an impact on the BRICS, which I was told existed from your development in concept, was to get an agenda to nationalize education. To me that is the core problem of economics and class. So, I think, my mentality, as it has been over the years, is to pursue that channel. Voting for whomever doesn't change anything because these people have their own networks, their own concepts, and this situation is creating a catastrophe throughout the world.

So to spend energy to remove an individual, to me,

is not really the best strategy; the best thing is to find an agenda where nobody can say "no." And nobody can say "no" to a balanced education that's nationalized and makes everybody equal, and taste the same thing.

If you want to deviate, you can do that in addition to the core, but we're falling behind because we do not have the quality of mentality to be able to run a country without people playing the ping pong game with politics.

LaRouche: That's true, but I would question what your appreciation is of the problem. Because the point of fact is, you don't want to have a standard educational program. And we're talking about an educational program because the educational program is the thing that defines what people are able to understand. That is, really understand, and understand in principle.

Now, what has happened, in the course of the Twentieth Century and beyond: Remember we're now beyond the Twentieth Century; we're in the Twentieth Century-plus, and the Twentieth Century-plus is characterized by idiocy. So we don't want to get into the idiocy department. But no, mankind does not understand mankind himself. There is a higher standard which must be applied.

The higher standard is defined by the fact that mankind,—people believe that their body talks for them, and it's the mere use of the voice, of that body that defines them. Well that ain't true. Because mankind is not something on Earth. Mankind is not intrinsically an earthling.

Now we live biologically, conveniently, in that kind of medium. But! the secret of mankind's progress—and this is what the question is—is what are the changes in behavior that must be introduced, to enable mankind to reach the levels of achievement which mankind urgently requires? And therefore, we need to take the whole school system down, in its present form, because the school system as I experienced it, even as a child, was rot and nonsense! And the only reason I had some intelligence, was because I didn't believe any of that garbage that I was taught to speak.

And therefore, the question is, mankind is not an earthling. Mankind's destiny belongs to the galaxies, it belongs to the astronomical realm, away from Earth as such. And it's the ability of mankind to see what that future of mankind is, in terms of higher systems. And therefore, what you have to do, is develop the creative powers of humanity, not how to imitate some kind of jazz.

… OK, you've got a couple of cases here. You've got, first of all, Brunelleschi. Now, Brunelleschi's work is probably the foundation of all modern Classical art. Now, that leads into other things. It leads into the work of Kepler. It goes beyond Kepler, and at the same time it goes into Shakespeare. Shakespeare's greatest work was actually a humanistic view. It was not a playwright view, not a drama as such. It was much deeper. And, if you look at the whole work of Shakespeare, you find you're reaching into something, which is much broader than any simple playwright design. This is an insight into the nature of mankind.

And you have other cases, and these cases are steps of progress, of scientific progress. And that progress is what we should actually be teaching people in schools. To become acquainted with modern history. And you start where? With Brunelleschi. Because Brunelleschi was the greatest scientist of that time.

See, you start with that. Then you go with other higher levels of people who followed him. You go on into Shakespeare, and Shakespeare very soon plays a very important role. And it's not just as a playwright: It's a conception of the study of the nature of man, and man's future and destiny. Then, we go from there into the other aspects of the struggle, which must always try to go beyond what mankind has achieved so far.

But we depend largely on that, and that's what education of children, education of students, is,—to give them an understanding of a process of history. And to be able to explain what that is, and to get people to respond, and to have insight into what these achievements really meant. And, what you're talking about is, I think, that question. And, that question is a very important one.

We must go deeply into at least modern history, beginning with the case of Brunelleschi, who is really the first systemic scientist in modern history. And so you start with him, and what was the great period of the Renaissance. And you go into the following period of evil. And Shakespeare was living against a period of evil, in his century. And then explain that, and then you say, "What's the lesson we, as students, or children, have to learn, to begin to understand what all of this means?"

What you're doing is in that direction, and I think that's precious for that reason.

When Californians Were Heroes

by Andrea Ingraham

Jan. 8—Unlike the dismal state of California politics today, where no one from either political party has challenged the genocidal policies and outlook espoused by Jerry Brown and Barack Obama, California politics was not always that way. During the first decade of its statehood, California politics was characterized by a life-or-death battle over slavery and the union, and the effort to civilize and uplift the population.

A state constitution which included a ban on slavery was submitted to Congress in 1849. For nine months a war in Congress ensued, as the southern Senators refused to upset the balance of 15 slave- and 15 free-states. A compromise crafted by Henry Clay resulted in California's admission on Sept. 9, 1850, avoiding civil war for the moment, but the slavocracy had by no means surrendered.

The leader of the Slave Power faction in California was William McKendree Gwin, a slave owner from Mississippi and protégé of Andrew Jackson; he was elected as one of the state's two first Senators. Gwin was determined to run the Democratic Party in the state, and under the Pierce Administration, he became controller of the patronage, giving him great power in the Party. His minions in the State legislature promoted many schemes, such as a bill to exclude free blacks from the state, a tough fugitive slave law, a bill to impose a stiff tax on foreign miners, a bill to legalize Chinese coolie contract labor, and a scheme to split the state in two, creating a southern California territory open to slavery.

In the U.S. Senate, Gwin and his colleague voted consistently with the southerners. By the end of the decade, on the eve of the Civil War, there was a strong sentiment that if the southern states seceded from the Union, California should secede and "form a separate republic."

Library of Congress

California Congressman David C. Broderick

Gwin's nemesis was a fierce fighter from Manhattan, New York named David Broderick. Broderick, the son of a skilled Irish stonecutter, was educated and recruited to politics by Townsend Harris[1] in Manhattan, and became a leader there of a Democratic Party organization of mostly Irish volunteer firefighters and street fighters. Soon after being defeated in a Congressional race due to sabotage from the Party elites, he left New York with some friends for California in 1849. Some went for the gold; Broderick went for the political fight, and built a political machine in San Francisco modeled on that of New York. In 1850 he was elected to the State Senate, where he waged fight after fight against the legislation proposed by the pro-southern, aka "Chivalry" Democrats.

In 1857, Broderick was elected to the U.S. Senate, where he soon found himself in a head-to-head battle with the Buchanan Administration he had helped to elect. The hottest issue of the day was the bill to admit Kansas under a fraudulently contrived pro-slavery state constitution, which Buchanan was vehemently promoting. In his first speech in the Senate, the new Senator ignored all protocol and denounced the President in no uncertain terms, saying: "...I do not intend, because I am a member of the Democratic party, to permit the President of the United States, who has been elected by that party, to create civil war in Kansas...."[2]

The following year Broderick split the Democratic Party in California, creating what became known as the Anti-Lecompton, or anti-Administration Democratic

---

1. Townsend Harris, a believer in education for all classes of people, was the founder of the City College of New York. He later became the first Consul General to Japan.
2. John C. Rives, excerpted from the *Congressional Globe: First session of the 35th Congress*, 1858, p. 164.

Party, and in 1859 he stumped the state campaigning for his slate, waging war on the pro-slavery Lecompton Democrats. Early in the campaign, Broderick was challenged to a duel for a supposed insult by the Chief Justice of the State Supreme Court, David Terry. Broderick refused to retract his truthful remarks. His slate, despite a vigorous canvass and last minute coalition with the Republicans, was defeated, and five days later Broderick was assassinated by way of a duel. His dying words were, "I die because I opposed a corrupt administration and the extension of slavery." Terry would soon return to his native Texas and recruit a Confederate regiment.

San Francisco Classical music and theater impresario Thomas Maguire

The Power of Music

Although Broderick's political movement contained many people from quite diverse backgrounds, in San Francisco the core of his political machine was made up of former New Yorkers. One of these was Tom Maguire, an individual who had been a close friend of Broderick's in Manhattan, and preceded him to San Francisco by several months.

Once in San Francisco, Maguire proceeded to launch an all-out cultural war. He opened a saloon, and upstairs built a theater, where he began drawing in opera singers, starting in 1849, in the wildest days of the gold rush. Maguire had been a carriage hack driver stationed at the Park Theater in Manhattan, where he developed a love for the theater, working later as a bartender there.

In 1849, the Verdi aria, 'Ernani! Ernani, involami,' was sung in Maguire's Jenny Lind Theater above his saloon, and Verdi became an instant sensation. Maguire, a semi-literate Irishman, began recruiting celebrity sopranos and others from around the world, increasingly throughout the decade. In 1851 he brought in the Booth family, and *Hamlet*, *Macbeth*, and *King Lear* were performed in that year. By 1859, the first full opera, *Il*

Edward D. Baker, who served in both the U.S. House of Representatives and U.S. Senate, was the founder of the California Republican Party.

Trovatore, was performed, and was an instant sensation, with 20,000 tickets sold for eleven performances. *Ernani*, *La Traviata*, and *Attila* were performed by end of summer.

The following year it was *Lucia di Lammermoor*, *La Traviata*, *Ernani*, and *Rigoletto*. There were 129 major productions, with about 1,500 tickets sold for each, totaling 217,500, to a population of 60,000, mostly gold miners who otherwise would spend their time and money in gambling houses and brothels. For 30 years, Maguire continued this effort, with stunning success, despite fires and bankruptcies and many other setbacks; eventually he built 12 theaters and a music academy.

Once he was quoted saying, "I lost $50,000 this year, but didn't I give them opera, eh?"

Edward Baker & Thomas Starr King

Broderick was not the only one in California who would risk life and limb to create a civilized state and save the union. Edward D. Baker, the great friend of Abraham Lincoln, orator, lawyer, statesman, and soldier, was another. A founder of the Republican Party in California, and leader of the pro-union, anti-slavery cause, he fought to ally with the Broderick Democrats against the Lecomptonites, and the one to whom those last words of Broderick were spoken. Baker delivered the oration at Broderick's funeral before an immense audience. He challenged them:

…Who now shall speak for California? Who be the interpreter of the wants of the Pacific Coast? Who can appeal to the communities of the Atlantic who love free labor? Who can speak for masses of men with a passionate love for the classes from whence he sprung? Who can defy the blandishments of power, the insolence of office, the corruption of administrations? What hopes are buried with him in the grave?

In his legal career in San Francisco, Baker took up many unpopular causes. In one case, he defended a gambler who had shot and killed a U.S. Marshall. The whole city was whipped up in a lynch mob frenzy against the gambler. In his summation to the jury, Baker said,

> The profession to which we belong is, of all others, fearless of public opinion. It has ever stood up against the tyranny of monarchs on the one hand, and the tyranny of public opinion on the other ... there is no wretch so steeped in all the agonies of vice and crime, that I would not have a heart to listen to his cry, and a tongue to speak in his defense, though around his head all the wrath of public opinion should gather, and rage, and roar, and roll, as the ocean rolls around the rock. And if I ever forget, if I ever deny, that highest duty of my profession, may God palsy this arm and hush my voice forever. . . .

Baker was elected to the U.S. Senate from Oregon in October 1860. On his way to Washington, D.C., he stopped in San Francisco where in a mass meeting, he uplifted the crowd to such an extent that the Democratic state delivered a plurality for Lincoln a few weeks later. In the Senate, he did more in his short tenure to demolish the arguments of the slave power ideologues than anyone else, and was Lincoln's most crucial ally in pushing his war measures through.

Following Lincoln's call to arms, Baker traveled to Manhattan, where he delivered a thrilling speech at a mass rally of 100,000 at Union Square, and recruited a regiment of former residents of California and Oregon, for which he was Colonel. He was killed in the first battle at Balls Bluff near Leesburg, Virginia. In more than one reported discussion, he had expressed the view that he did not expect to live long, but rather to fall while leading his inexperienced regiment, and would be content if he did.[3]

Yet another hero of that day was the Reverend

Thomas Starr King, leader of the fight to keep California in the Union during the Civil War.

Thomas Starr King. Born in Manhattan, raised in Boston, the son of a mechanic-turned-minister of the Unitarian Church, King at a young age had gained a reputation as a gifted speaker and preacher and was recruited by Dr. Henry W. Bellows, pastor of the All Souls Unitarian Church in New York City, to pastor the First Unitarian Church in San Francisco in 1860. Known for his profound and uplifting speeches such as "Substance and Show," "Socrates," "Beethoven," and "Sight and Insight" (which proved the fallacy of sense perception and the greatness of the human mind), King's input was much needed in California, but he soon found he was destined for an even greater role.

After the outbreak of the Civil War, and especially after the death of Baker, Starr King took it upon himself to ensure that California remained true to the Union. In addition to the speeches and sermons he brought from the East, he added a whole new repertoire of fiercely patriotic speeches, defending the Union, the revolution, Lincoln, and emancipation, fearlessly exhorting his listeners. In addition, he became the key collaborator of Dr. Bellows, who by this time had established the Sanitary Commission, the forerunner of the Red Cross, created to provide support for sick and injured Union soldiers. King traveled tirelessly throughout California and Oregon, speaking and fundraising for this cause, such that California contributed more money to the Sanitary Commission than any other state. By 1864, the tide of the war turning, he had worn down his already fragile body, and died, probably of diphtheria, at the age of 40.

* * *

Residents of California today have no excuse to accept the degenerate "Californication," as Lyndon LaRouche so aptly names the popular culture today, nor do citizens elsewhere. Rather, let us take the great assets of the state—its huge population of many nationalities, its agricultural capability to feed the world, its access to the Pacific rim—and lead the country into the future. As Baker said in an address in San Francisco celebrating the success of the Atlantic telegraph cable, "Here all people and all tongues shall meet. Here shall be a more perfect civilization . . . ."

Let us kick out Jerry Brown now!

---

3. For more on Baker and Broderick, see https://www.dropbox.com/s/xazi3f2qsramfr6/BAKER.pdf?dl=0 and https://www.dropbox.com/s/1ai19qvric22cet/BRODERICK.pdf?dl=0

Beauty Is Necessary for Mankind

During the Jan. 8th LaRouche PAC Webcast, the following exchange took place, wherein the subject of creating a new Renaissance was posed.

Matthew Ogden: During our discussion earlier this afternoon with Helga Zepp-LaRouche, she emphatically stressed that there is no escape from this Dark Age, this looming Dark Age, of war and economic disintegration, short of the initiation of an entirely new paradigm for civilization, one which makes a clean break with the failed policies of the past, and literally intends to usher in a New Renaissance on the scale of what we saw with the great European Golden Renaissance of several centuries ago, but really going much, much further beyond this, to reach accomplishments that mankind has not achieved before.

That's the kind of vision of the new paradigm, which, over the past several months and years, Helga Zepp-LaRouche has personally been touring the world discussing, and the LaRouche movement has been engaged in: not just talking about the necessity of bringing this about, but actively engaged in creating the new paradigm. . . .

The major aspect of the creation of a new paradigm, which really hinges on which way the United States goes in the coming days and months, is the active intervention of the LaRouche movement and its activists into New York City, specifically into Manhattan. The spear-point of this, which has become known as the Manhattan Project, has been a broad-based campaign for the revival of great Classical culture, specifically great Classical music in the form of choral singing. Now, this project has rapidly developed in a qualitative way, as marked by the most recent series of concerts of Handel's *Messiah*, which took place

over the weekend of Dec. 19th and 20th. These two concerts were co-sponsored by the Schiller Institute Community Chorus and the Foundation for the Revival of Classical Culture.

The first of these concerts was in Brooklyn on Dec. 19, and the second, the following day in Manhattan at the Unitarian Church of All Souls on the Upper East Side. The full video recordings of both of these concerts now are available on YouTube, and we encourage you to watch them if you have not already done so, and absolutely to circulate them as widely as you can. It's one of the greatest gifts you can give to your friends and relatives; but what we're going to do right now is to treat you to a few clips from the second of those concerts, the Manhattan performance, as a prelude to the remarks that Megan Beets is going to make in the next segment of our webcast here tonight.

The *Messiah* Performances

Excerpts were then played from the Manhattan concert, including "For Unto Us a Child Is Born," "Surely He Hath Borne Our Griefs," and the "Hallelujah!" chorus.

Megan Beets: What you just got a taste of, is the leading and most essential edge of our political move-

Schiller Institute

John Sigerson conducting the Schiller Institute chorus at the Dec. 19, 2015 performance of Handel's Messiah *at the Sacred Hearts & St. Stephen Roman Catholic Church in Brooklyn.*

ment's intervention into the United States at this time. It represents the fruits of roughly one year of intense work of building the Schiller Institute New York Community Chorus, which is formed of some professionals and semi-professionals, but mostly amateurs, political organizers, political supporters of the LaRouche movement and others, who joined the chorus, many of whom had no prior musical experience.

This chorus is singing at the scientifically correct tuning of "A" at 432—lower than most choruses and orchestras around the world—and its members are trained or are training in the Classical tradition of the Italian Bel Canto school. What you just saw and heard, represents a year of intense work, intense dedication; the commitment of long hours on the part of the organizers of the chorus; and the commitment of resources in many forms—financial, time resources, and so forth.

Now, given the picture of the world strategic situation that Jeff just presented, and given the fact that this movement—upon which and upon whose leadership the fate of the United States, and really the world, depends—is rather small and limited in resources, one could ask, "Shouldn't we direct our very limited resources somewhere else, somewhere more precisely focused on the fight at hand? Shouldn't we send more people to Congress? Shouldn't we not waste our resources on something so impractical, and so indirectly related to the timely fight at hand?" No.

Nothing Practical Will Help

It's precisely in the fact that the formation and activity of the chorus is not practical that you get a taste of where the victory lies. Nothing "practical" can change the United States at this point, and it's not just the fact that Classical music and this chorus is not practical. That's not the important point. The point is that it's beautiful; beauty, beautiful culture, is not a luxury for mankind. It's a necessary and essential condition for humanity, and in fact, it's the only way in which we can change the country and have a possibility of winning this political fight.

I want people to just think for a second; look around you, think about the culture today, the popular culture. The popular culture of the West especially has become so degraded, so depraved. Over the course of the Twentieth Century, the culture has become, step by step, worse and worse. There's nothing human left. There's nothing universal left in film, in drama, in the popular

music. And in that, I'm also including the popular expressions of so-called Classical music.

Ugliness, Emptiness, and Frivolity

The culture today celebrates ugliness, sex, banality, emptiness, and frivolity. It glorifies the worst and most low and empty tendencies in man. All of those characteristics of the popular culture have dulled the sensibilities, and the sensitivities, of people in our society to be able to be moved by high, new, and beautiful important ideas.

Now that really gets to the essential point. We're not in this political civilizational crisis because of a lack of knowing what to do. The solutions are there. The options are there. We have identified exactly what steps must be taken, and they will work. The political power to put them into effect is there. What's lacking is the will and morality in the culture to make it happen.

This is the essential question: How do we reawaken that will, and that morality, within society? How do you restore to a people a sense of their humanity?

So, here, I'd like to bring in some thoughts from the work of somebody who hardly any Americans are familiar with, and that is the great poet of freedom, Friedrich Schiller, who was German, and who lived at the very end of the Eighteenth and beginning of the Nineteenth Centuries. Schiller lived during a very tumultuous time politically. In 1794, he authored a series of letters which address very precisely, and also very scientifically, exactly this question at hand.

This was right about the time that Schiller watched, with great horror, the collapse of the French Revolution, which had held so much hope and potential for the continuation of the American Revolution, and the political freedom of Europe, and then all the world. Schiller saw it collapse into brutality and violence, and eventually it collapsed into fascism, under the rule of Napoleon. And in response to that, Schiller said, "A great moment has found a little people."

Ennobling a Degraded People

What he presents in these letters, from which I'd like to read a couple of short excerpts, is that the only means of freeing mankind from the kind of tragedy that was witnessed in the French Revolution, and in many prior attempts—and in the situation we find ourselves in today—the only means of freeing mankind is nothing practical, nothing currently existing within mankind, within society. You have to create a new potential within mankind. And Schiller said the only way to do this, is through beautiful art.

I'd like to read short excerpts, and I'm going to begin with a passage where Schiller identifies exactly what I just identified a couple of minutes ago: that the problem is not a lack of knowledge. He says: "From whence arises this still so universal predominance of prejudices, and this darkness of thought, with all the light which philosophy and experience have shed on it? The age is enlightened; that is to say, knowledge has been discovered and made public, which would suffice to at least rectify our practical principles. The spirit of free inquiry has dispelled the erroneous conceptions which blocked the access to truth for a long time, and reason has purified itself of the illusions of the senses, and deceitful sophistry. So why is it that we are still barbarians?"

To that, Schiller says: "You must dare to be wise. Energetic courage is needed to overcome the obstacles which the inertia of nature and of cowardice of heart place in opposition to our enlightenment. It is significant that the ancient myth has the goddess of wisdom emerge fully armed from Jupiter's head. For her first action is warlike."

Then Schiller warns: "But, people would already have to be wise in order to love wisdom. Therefore it is not enough to conclude that any enlightenment of the understanding only deserves our respect insofar as it affects the character in turn. To a certain extent, it must proceed from the character, because the way to the head must be opened by the heart. The development of the capacity for feeling is the more urgent need of our age: not only because it will be a means of making improved insights effective for practical life, but for the very reason that it awakens this improvement of insight."

But How?

Now, how do we accomplish this? How do we develop within a population a disgust for depravity, and a true ennoblement of the capacity for feeling?

Schiller says that the tool to do this is art, is beautiful art. He says: "Art, like science, is free from everything that is practical and is established by human conven-

pinehurst19475

A statue of the Poet of Freedom Friedrich Schiller in Belle Isle, Detroit, Michigan. It was erected in 1908.

tion, and both rejoice in an absolute immunity from human lawlessness. The political legislator can enclose their territory, but he cannot govern within it. He can outlaw a friend of truth, but the truth exists. He can humiliate the artist, but he cannot degrade art."

So, then, how do you win over a degraded people, or even an underdeveloped, undeveloped people, to choose reason? He says: "People's taste is purely in their hearts. In vain you will assail their maxims. In vain you will condemn their deeds. But you can try your fashioning hand on their idleness. Drive away lawlessness, frivolity, and brutality from their entertainment, and you will imperceptibly banish it from their actions, and finally, from their character. Where you find them, surround them with noble, great, and ingenious forms. Place the symbols of excellence all around them until reality is overcome by appearance, and nature is overcome by art."

Now Schiller makes the point more precisely a little bit later in the series of letters, that in order to capture truth, you have to venture out beyond what he calls reality, beyond what currently exists. And you have to venture out into the imagination to capture something which is true. And that's really the purpose of great art: to remove from mankind the limitations and the imperfections which he currently suffers, even if it's only for the short duration of the performance or viewing of the piece of art. And during that segment of time, during the experience and the process of participating in beautiful culture and beautiful art, man's emotions, man's passions and desires, can be brought into coherence with reason, with what is true, what is just, and what is good.

What Was the Secret in Manhattan?

That is the task and the power of art: to elevate mankind as much as possible to the ideal. And to put him into a condition where his impulses, his free will, and the laws of man are so ennobled that they can be relied upon as a force of nature. Now, with that in mind, return to the concert that you saw a glimpse of at the beginning.

The day after the concert, on Monday, Dec. 21, during the Policy Committee show, Mr. LaRouche responded to what had happened in Manhattan; he said: "What happened in these concerts was something which was music, but it was not just music *per se*. It's the way that the human mind functions competently. It was a process which gave over 1,000 people—who participated both in the audience and as musicians—it gave them an experience of a resonance with the human mind." That's art; that's the purpose of art. To develop, to experience, and to celebrate that capacity of true creativity in mankind.

Now, given that, it's no wonder that if we look back in history, we see that in great periods of political progress and political development for mankind, we've always had the companion of the development of great art. We saw that in the Golden Renaissance of Italy, where simultaneously we had the development of the beginnings of the sovereign nation-state, and the developments in poetry and art and singing. It's no wonder that Mozart was a stern supporter of the American Revolution; Beethoven likewise. It's no surprise that Giuseppe Verdi was a supporter of the movement for sovereignty in Italy, and also served in the Italian Senate. That Johannes Brahms was a great supporter of Bismarck, who was the bastion against the takeover of Europe by the British Empire. And it's no wonder that even from a young age, Lyndon LaRouche has understood and taken great pleasure and joy in, and promoted the restoration and the renaissance of Classical art.

Now, return in your mind to what Jeff laid out, to the

www.rockhellradio.com

How can today's culture of ugliness and degradation be replaced?

great political crisis at hand, and the task ahead of us in the short term, which is to oppose the great evil which has taken over the planet—that is, the British Empire and its stooge in the person of Barack Obama. As Mr. LaRouche said, we have gained a foothold against that evil with what was done in Manhattan. And I'd like to end by both challenging and also inviting all of you to take up the full scope of that fight against evil.

We're not going to win part of the battle; this is not a fight for an issue. If you fight for an issue, we will lose. Ironically, the only fight that can be won at this point is the big one, is the whole fight, the fight for a completely new paradigm. Fight for a new, uplifted ennobled state of mankind, in which man is taking a great step forward toward fulfilling his ideal and his true potential. And if you're in the New York area, you can start by joining the chorus.

Join the Chorus!

At the LaRouche PAC Jan. 9th Manhattan Town Hall Meeting, John Sigerson, the conductor of the Schiller Institute New York Community Chorus, delivered the following remarks, partially in response to what Megan Beets had said the previous day concerning the continuing work of that chorus.

John Sigerson: It would be a big mistake to think that the choral work, the chorus, is some kind of soft way of getting people into the hard core of the LaRouche movement, or something like that. That would

Classical beauty in music and sculpture, as conveyed in one of the many bas reliefs on the choir lofts by Luca della Robbia in Brunelleschi's Florence cathedral.

be a stupid way of looking at it, and I think that if anybody had any doubts about that, they should simply watch the video of the two concerts that we did on Dec. 19th and 20th. How many people were at the concert or have heard it? Those of you who haven't, please, get on the website and watch this.

I was lucky enough last night, to listen to part of the webcast that was done by Jeff Steinberg and Megan Beets, which is on the website also, and in which, after a very powerful presentation by Jeff, Megan Beets gets up and gives just as powerful a presentation of the significance of what was done on Dec. 19th and 20th. And frankly, even though I was the conductor of these events, I was very surprised at seeing what we accomplished.

Handel's *Messiah* is performed probably more frequently than any other work. But nevertheless, the response that we got with these two concerts was something quite remarkable. And I think it's useful for everyone to consider exactly what it was that created that kind of effect.

Bringing People to a Higher Plane

I think it's very similar to the effect that Brunelleschi had when he created the famous dome on the Cathedral of Santa Maria del Fiore in Florence, Italy. It's a question of continuous curvature. That is, I don't know how many of you have heard many performances of Handel's *Messiah*; it's done all the time. It's done terribly, in my view, most of the time. With great gusto! So that I don't think it was the gusto that was what moved the audience.

It's not that. It was this question of the curvature, which is that, even though we weren't saying anything explicitly about all of the things that were discussed here today, it was informed by all of those things. And the being informed, is what created that kind of curvature for everyone, in exactly the way that Friedrich Schiller describes in his *Aesthetical Letters.* It brings people in a way that they don't even understand, onto a higher plane. And I think everybody felt that.

Now, how did we do it? Interesting question. And how can it be done? Well, part of it has to do with Lyndon LaRouche and his influence on me personally and the people we've been working with. I spent many an hour, and continue to do so, comparing the performances by the greatest conductor and creative musician of the Twentieth Century, Wilhelm Furtwängler, to other recordings. He died when I was three years old, so I didn't have a chance to hear him live. I've pondered, over and over again, what's the difference between what Furtwängler was able to do with audiences, and with performances, and what virtually everyone else has done. I would say that other performances have flashes of what Furtwängler does, but there is that "certain something" that Furtwängler was able to sustain; and I've dedicated my life to being able to create that "certain something."

And that's exactly what organizing people is all about as well, in terms of changing their ways of thinking, by changes in curvature of thought, in ways that they may not even perceive, initially. And things grow and grow and grow. And I think that's exactly what we're doing with the chorus right now. And we hope to continue it. The chorus should also grow, and grow, and grow.

So, if you haven't joined, join! And if you *have* joined, I think it would be good for you to take out any old recording you've got of the *Messiah* and compare it to what we did. And think for yourselves, exactly what was that difference? See if you can put your finger on it.

The British Agenda Behind the Tenth Amendment Movement

by Kesha Rogers

Kesha Rogers is a member of the LaRouche PAC Policy Committee.

Jan. 12—The British Empire and its ilk must be defeated once and for all, and the true fight for human freedom and creativity—which our founding fathers understood was the key battle in the establishment of our nation and the principles embodied in our Constitution—must be restored.

This week marked the 14th Annual "Policy Orientation" for the Texas State Legislature, a conference sponsored by the Texas Public Policy Foundation (TPPF). This conference was a continuation of what *EIR* and the LaRouche movement have fought against for many decades now,— the plot by the British Royals to balkanize the United States,[1] and devolve the nation-state to British colonial control.

This intention was expressed throughout the TPPF conference, but most emphatically in the final keynote speech given by Texas Governor Greg Abbott. Speaking before over a thousand participants and several dozen media outlets, Abbott criticized the "overreach" of the federal government and declared that, "If we want to solve the problems we face today, we need to fix the fractured foundation of the country."

During his speech, Abbott unveiled what he called the Texas Plan. The plan includes Constitutional amendments "to put teeth into the Tenth Amendment," which states: "The powers not delegated to the United States by the Constitution, nor prohibited by it to the

Convention of States Project

Texas Governor Greg Abbott keynoting the Texas Public Policy Foundation's Annual Policy Orientation on Jan. 8, on his plans to devolve the Constitution.

States, are reserved to the States respectively, or to the people."

A Gramm-Sized Brain

The Texas Plan is part of an ongoing and growing call for a convention of states to amend the Constitution. Abbott calls for the introduction of several amendments. He attacks the Supreme Court as a "co-conspirator in the abandonment of the U.S. Constitution." He says that the Supreme Court has hamstrung the states' ability to enforce the Tenth Amendment. In his speech, Abbott even had the audacity to cite Alexander Hamilton and Ben Franklin as authorities for this British Plan for the devolution of the United States and our nation's republic.

At the end of his speech, Abbott fraudulently cited Hamilton: "Alexander Hamilton wrote our Constitution, beginning with the phrase, 'We the people ....'" Someone forgot to tell the Governor that that phrase continues, "We the People of the United States, in Order

---

1. "The British Royals Plot to Balkanize the United States," by Kathleen Klenetsky, *EIR*, Volume 22, Number 23, June 2, 1995.

to form a more perfect Union, . . .," not we the people of Texas. The fight against such insane proposals that Abbott—and others of British ilk throughout the United States—continue to push, goes to the root of defending the ideas expressed in our U.S. Declaration of Independence, which stands at the center of the battle of truly human freedom and happiness.

That expression of human freedom was not about the free market, private property, or states' rights. The fight has been for true human creativity. The principles so identified in our Declaration are those of Life, Liberty, and the Pursuit of Happiness, as opposed to John Locke's slavery-centered idea of the pursuit of property, which views human beings as animals, not rational and creative beings.

No one should be shocked by Abbott's British-centered plan, which spits in the faces of Hamilton and Franklin. It has been the intention of the British Empire since the inception of our republic, that the United States would be dissolved, and that the states would be colonies of the British once again. It has also been the intention of the British monarchy to reduce the world's population to less than one billion people. Among the key institutions and networks that have been the promoters of this evil British plot, have been those associated with the so-called Conservative Revolution of Newt Gingrich and Phil Gramm,— or what would be better expressed as the states' rights crowd's push for conservative devolution.

Who are the key names of destruction and evil at the head of the Texas Public Policy Foundation (TPPF), working on behalf of the British Empire? They are its Chairman, Dr. Wendy Gramm, and her husband, former U.S. Senator Phil Gramm. These two have been working in accord with the British Royals for many years, pushing policies of deregulation, for which Wendy Gramm was known in her role as the Chairman of the U.S. Commodity Futures Trading Commission from 1988 to 1993. Her husband, the notorious Phil Gramm, is a member of the Newt Gingrich posse in the Conservative Revolution, and the destructive mind behind the 1999 take-down of the Glass-Steagall Act, enacted in

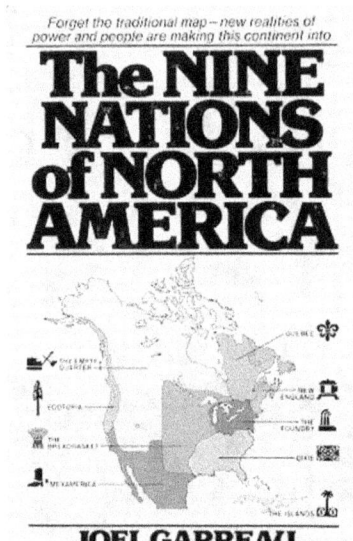

The long-standing British plan to split up the United States has been championed by "liberals" and "conservatives" alike. This book by then-Washington Post writer Joel Garreau was published in 1981.

1933 under the leadership of President Franklin Roosevelt.

I spoke with Phil Gramm following the luncheon. I told him that he should be indicted for his role in the UBS and Crédit Suisse tax fraud and money laundering, and for aiding al-Qaeda. He denied any association with any of them and played ignorant, saying he knew nothing about what I was saying. I then asked him about his decision to repeal Glass-Steagall, to which he replied that it was the right one, that even Bill Clinton said it was the right decision, and that no one has been able to prove that the "recession" was the result of repealing Glass-Steagall.

Reality Enters

Governor Abbott did not just pull his insane plan to tear apart the very foundation that holds our Union together from thin air. It has become the continued and ongoing agenda of the British Empire and its states' rights cronies. The Gingrich revolution has been closely tied to organizations such as the American Legislative Exchange Council (ALEC), founded in 1973, at the same as the Heritage Foundation. ALEC has been described as the grassroots arm of the Conservative Revolution against the American System.[2]

During the TPPF conference, there was a strong push by presenters to implement the anti-American System ideas of the "free market," as the basis for so-called individual freedoms. One of the presenters, a Texas State Senator, projected a quotation from Milton Friedman on the screen to anchor her argument against the "overreach" of the federal government: "Underlying most arguments against the free market is the lack of belief in freedom itself."

During a panel titled, "How will Texas Protect Its Citizens from the National Debt Crisis?" the speakers asked: If the money and economy crash, what does Texas have in place to protect itself? "Texas has to be prepared to take care of its citizens," said one panelist, "If the Fed crashes or not, Texas has to be prepared."

During this panel discussion, I intervened from the

---

2. "States Rights Crowd Pushes the Conservative Devolution," by Nancy Spannaus, *ibid.*

floor. stating that our Constitution was founded on the principles established by our first Treasury Secretary, Alexander Hamilton, and given in its Preamble, which begins, "We the People of the United States, in Order to form a more perfect Union...." We have gotten further and further away from that more perfect union, I said, and the policies being pushed in the panel were the cause of this division.

I added that the entire financial system is bankrupt; the people of this state and this nation are in deep despair; and record unemployment and increasing suicide have taken over. There is no local solution that will fix the problem. Consider that Europe is already being torn apart by the murderous bail-in policy. I showed that Obama and the Congress have already written bail-in into law under the Dodd-Frank Act, and that it is ready to be unleashed here in the United States. I made made clear that the bail-in demonstrates the idiocy of all local "solutions," exposing them as frauds to divert and rile people up, while leaving them vulnerable to death.

The panelists tried to turn the question away from the need for a national solution to the question of the crash of the stock market, but some in the audience understood the seriousness of these remarks and asked what could be done.

Several people came up thanking me for my comments afterwards, and some agreed that the solution is Glass-Steagall. Others wanted to know who will repeal Dodd-Frank.

As we celebrate the birthday of Alexander Hamilton this week, we must embrace the true principles of happiness and freedom as defined in our U.S. Declaration of Independence, and the natural law of our divine Creator that express the creative powers of mankind. We must once and for all rid the nation of the grip of the British Empire and its Wall Street, and restore the true unity of our nation based on the divine principles of natural law which Hamilton so profoundly understood, and as he expressed them in the following remarks made in 1775:

> To grant, that there is a supreme intelligence, who rules the world, and has established laws to regulate the actions of his creatures; and still, to assert that man, in a state of nature, may be considered as perfectly free from all restraints of *law and government*, appear to a common understanding altogether irreconcilable.
>
> Good and wise men, in all ages, have em-

braced a very dissimilar theory. They have supposed that the deity, from the relations, we stand in, to himself and to each other, has constituted an eternal and immutable law, which is, indispensably, obligatory upon all mankind, prior to any human institution whatever.

This is what is called the law of nature....

Upon this law, depend the natural rights of mankind, the supreme being gave existence to man, together with the means of preserving and beatifying that existence. He endowed him with rational faculties, by the help of which, to discern and pursue such things, as were consistent with his duty and interest, and invested him with an inviolable right to personal liberty, and personal safety....

The sacred rights of mankind are not to be rummaged for, among old parchments, or musty records. They are written, as with a sun beam, in the whole *volume* of human nature, by the hand of the divinity itself; and can never be erased or obscured by mortal power.[3]

---

3. Alexander Hamilton, "The Farmer Refuted," February 23, 1775.

Obama Escalates War Confrontation with China Over North Korean Nuclear Test

by Carl Osgood

Jan. 11—On Jan. 6, 2016, the government of North Korea announced that it had carried out a successful nuclear test at its facility in Punggye-ri, in a remote area in the northeast of the country, and that the test had been successful in detonating a miniaturized hydrogen bomb.

The issue before us is not the North Korean test. The only real strategic consideration is how that test will be used by the Obama Administration and its British Imperial controllers, to justify further provocations against China, further escalating the ongoing provocations designed to bring the world to a thermonuclear World War III.

The North Korean test comes in the context of the violent im-

DoD/Glenn Fawcett

U.S. Defense Secretary Ash Carter, then Deputy Secretary, meeting with the South Korean Defense Minister Kim Byung-kwan (right) in March 2013. The Obama Administration agenda then, as now, was to push South Korea to join in the missile defense "ring around China."

plosion of the trans-Atlantic financial system. The British Empire has no intention, as *EIR* Editor-in-Chief Lyndon LaRouche has repeatedly warned, of letting Asia or any other part of the planet survive that financial collapse. "The point is the intention of the British system, and it is the British system from the top down, and the system that is the cause of this process" of collapse, LaRouche said in remarks to colleagues on Jan. 5. "Now we have the case, in terms of Britain, and the British system setting up a global mass killing of the human population."

In reaction to the North Korean test, the immediate response from the Obama Administration was to blame China for it. On Jan. 7, Secretary of State John Kerry spoke to Chinese Foreign Minister Wang Yi, and then personally appeared in the State Department press briefing room. Kerry declared that he had warned Wang

that China's go-soft approach to influencing North Korea had proven a failure: "Today, in my conversation with the Chinese, I made it clear that [their approach] has not worked and we cannot continue business as usual."

China responded angrily to Kerry's suggestion the following day. Speaking at a press conference, Chinese Foreign Ministry spokeswoman Hua Chunying stated: "The origin and crux of the nuclear issue on the Korean Peninsula has never been China." China's *Global Times,* owned by the Communist Party's *People's Daily,* took an even tougher stance which was described by the *New York Times* as a "fiery rebuttal." The *Global Times* editorial stated that "in no way will China bear the responsibilities that the U.S., South Korea and Japan should take.... The hostilities between them and Pyongyang are actually the source of the nuclear problems. The China-North Korea relationship should not be dragged into antagonism."

Upping the Nuclear Ante

On Jan. 10, four days after the North Korean test, a U.S. B-52 strategic bomber was flown 1,900 miles, from Andersen Air Force Base on the island of Guam, to South Korea. There it was joined by four fighter aircraft to conduct flyovers and maneuvers near the Osan Air Force Base, a U.S. base in South Korea only 48 miles from the demilitarized zone separating the two Koreas.

Although U.S. officials refused to divulge whether the B-52 was carrying nuclear armaments, the aircraft is normally equipped with twelve AGM-86 air-launched nuclear cruise missiles, with yields of up to 150 kilotons each. The bomber is also normally equipped with a wide variety of conventional weapons, including up to fifty-one 500-pound unguided bombs, ten laser-guided bombs, or eight Harpoon anti-ship missiles. The fact that the B-52 is a nuclear capable aircraft, and was directly deployed on the North Korean border, is seen not only as a direct threat to North Korea, but to China as well.

These actions also come in a context where U.S. and South Korean defense officials have been in discussions about the further deployment of U.S. "strategic assets" to South Korea, likely to include an aircraft carrier (the USS Ronald Reagan is in port in Yokosuka, Japan), F-22 stealth fighters, and submarines. The United States is also pressuring Seoul to accept military deployments that it has resisted, for reasons of its relationship with China. The *Korea Herald* reported that the North's nuclear test could be used as a catalyst to strengthen the bilateral cooperation between the United States and Japan, and incorporate South Korea into Washington's efforts to build an anti-China integrated air and missile defense program, or IAMD.

Additionally, it is known that the United States has been pressuring South Korea to install an advanced missile defense asset, called the Terminal High Altitude Area Defense (THAAD), the ultimate target of which would be China.

On its part, the government of North Korea responded to the flyover by saying that it was an action destined to send the United States and North Korea to the "edge of war." It should also be kept in mind that memories of the Korean War, when the North Korean capital of Pyongyang was "flattened" and almost completely destroyed by American bomber aircraft, are still very much alive in the minds of today's North Korean leadership.

Some Cowardly, War-Mad Generals

Some elements of the senior leadership of the U.S. military are eagerly playing along with the provocations against Russia and China, unlike the former Chairman of the Joint Chiefs Gen. Martin Dempsey and his team, who fought them. On Jan. 5, Chief of Naval Operations Admiral John Richardson issued a paper advertised as his "blueprint for a stronger Navy," in which procuring a new fleet of ballistic-missile submarines is identified as his number one priority.

"This is foundational to our survival as a nation," Richardson's paper claims. "From a security standpoint in this day and age, a world-class nuclear capability" is required to be considered a great power, he told the Associated Press in a Dec. 31 interview. Without it, "we could be threatened or coerced by another nation who could hold this nuclear threat over our heads," he added. "If we don't reconstitute the undersea leg" of the nuclear triad, "then we're not even at the table to discuss world affairs as a great power."

The plan to replace the existing fleet of 14 Ohio-class ballistic missile submarines with twelve new boats, expected to begin entering service in the 2025 time-frame, is one part of a larger plan, estimated by the Congressional Budget Office to cost about $325 billion over 30 years. The plan includes a new bomber for the U.S. Air Force along with a new cruise missile, as well as replacement of the Air Force's fleet of Minuteman ICBMs.

Further excerpts from Richardson's plan are illuminating:

> For the first time in 25 years, the United States is facing a return to great power competition. Russia and China both seek to be global powers. Their goals are backed by a growing arsenal of high-end warfighting capabilities, many of which are focused specifically on our vulnerabilities, and are increasingly designed from the ground up to leverage the maritime, technological, and information systems.

Richardson states that one issue he wants to focus on is "gray warfare," an area that falls between peace and full armed conflict. It typically involves some ag-

U.S. Air Force/Michael J. Pausic

Gen. Philip Breedlove, Commander of the U.S. European Command and the Supreme Allied Commander Europe of NATO, speaking at an Air Force Association meeting in 2014.

gression or use of force, but is deliberately ambiguous in nature, "just below the level of conflict."

On the NATO Front

In Europe, General Philip Breedlove, commander of NATO and of U.S. European Command issued his own provocation in remarks as reported on Jan. 7. In comments to reporters in Stuttgart, Germany, Breedlove complained that the United States has "hugged the bear" for too long, and it's time to recognize that we are dealing with a revanchist Russia with aggressive tendencies. Breedlove met with Chairman of the Joint Chiefs of Staff Gen. Joseph Dunford when Dunford was in Stuttgart a couple of days before, and these remarks appear to have been made shortly after that meeting.

In what can only be described as wartime propaganda, Breedlove lied that it was Russian President Vladimir Putin who explicitly rejected the outstretched hand of friendship of the United States, stating: "What I would offer is that if you look at Russia's actions all the way back to '08—in Georgia, in Nagorno-Karabakh, in Crimea, in the Donbass, and now down in Syria—we see what most call a revanchist Russia that has put force back on the table as an instrument of national power to meet their objectives."

Breedlove also complained that the U.S. "force posture" in Europe has declined. He is now advocating a more "robust" U.S. military presence in Europe. He noted that the Army has begun deploying a brigade-sized unit to the region, along with 200 M1 Abrams tanks and additional vehicles and weapons.

Breedlove's ravings were actually contradicted by the semi-official analysis issued by the U.S. Army's *Military Review* in its most recent issue, released on Dec. 31. That issue published the full transcript of Russian President Vladimir Putin's remarks to the UN General Assembly on Sept. 28, as well as an article by Russian Chief of the General Staff Gen. Valery Gerasimov on the nature of future warfare, accompanied by an analysis by Charles K. Bartles, a Russian language specialist at the Army's Foreign Military Studies Office.

Lunatics like Breedlove have pointed to Gerasimov's article as proof of an operational Russian doctrine of "hybrid warfare," but in his analysis, Bartles refutes that notion, and demonstrates that what Gerasimov was actually describing was how he sees the future threat environment, a threat environment that includes NATO expansion, U.S.-led wars of regime change and so-called color revolutions.

The Seat of Responsibility

It is crystal clear that, whatever the line-up is of U.S. military leaders going along with the Obama Administration's war provocations against China and Russia, this situation only exists because the United States Congress, which has the responsibility to defend the U.S. Constitution against an out-of-control executive, has failed miserably in its Constitutional obligations.

It is cowardice, and cowardice alone, which is preventing members of Congress from taking action to remove President Obama from office either by impeachment or by invoking the 25th Amendment. Squirm as they might, the escalating threat of global warfare is a product of their own cowardice. Unless some of them decide to act, and soon, they will probably all find themselves dead some fine day, along with most of the rest of us. And with no Internet to tell them that Obama has just launched thermonuclear war.